The Practice of Social Work

General Editors: Bill Jordan and Jean Packman

Social Work, Justice and Control

Peter Raynor

Basil Blackwell

© Peter Raynor 1985

First published 1985

Basil Blackwell Ltd
108 Cowley Road, Oxford OX4 1JF, UK

Basil Blackwell Inc.
432 Park Avenue South, Suite 1505,
New York, NY 10016, USA

British Library Cataloguing in Publication Data

Raynor, Peter
Social work, justice and control.
—(The practice of social work; 13)
1. Probation—England
I. Title   II. Series
364.6'3'0942   HV9346.A5

ISBN 0-631-13731-9
ISBN 0-631-13732-7 Pbk

Library of Congress Cataloging in Publication Data

Raynor, Peter.
Social work, justice and control.
(The Practice of social work; 13)
Bibliography: p.
Includes index.
1. Social work with delinquents and criminals—
Great Britain.   2. Rehabilitation of criminals—
Great Britain.   3. Probation—Great Britain.
I. Title.   II. Series.
HV7428.R39   1985   365'.66'0941   85—7365
ISBN 0-631-13731-9
ISBN 0-631-13732-7 (pbk.)

Typeset by Pioneer, East Sussex
Printed in Great Britain by
Billing and Sons Ltd, Worcester

Contents

Acknowledgements

This book has been growing for some time in odd moments, and its eventual appearance owes much to the editorial encouragement of Bill Jordan and to a sense of urgency created by the 1982 Criminal Justice Act. Many colleagues and students within and outside the Probation Service have contributed to the development and testing of the ideas in it; particularly David Smith, Martin Seddon, Maurice Vanstone (who also read and commented on the manuscript), Deri Lewis (who encouraged me to take an interest in the Afan Alternative project), Howard Lewis (whose work in Seven Sisters provided further material for chapter 10), colleagues in the University College of Swansea, fellow members of the National Association of Victim Support Schemes, and others too numerous to mention individually. A particular intellectual debt is owed to Tony Bottoms and Bill McWilliams for their work on the 'non-treatment paradigm'. Any remaining errors or injustices are, of course, my own.

Thanks are also due to my employers at Swansea University for providing academic opportunities to develop my ideas, reinforced by the constant stimulus of lecture preparation. Some paradoxical acknowledgement is also owed to the unnamed officials of the Home Office and the Central Council for Education and Training in Social Work, whose as yet unexplained decision to withdraw financial aid from my probation students in the 1981 training cuts helped to stimulate a wider dissemination of the ideas on which their training had been based. I am grateful to the editors of the *British Journal of Social*

Work, the *Probation Journal* and *Social Work Today* for permission to use material which first appeared in their pages, and to Edna Owen, Maureen Short and Vera Quinn for typing the manuscript.

The quotations from Butler's 'Erewhon' are from the Penguin edition of 1935.

PART I

The Story So Far

It is a distinguishing characteristic of the Erewhonians
that when they profess themselves to be quite certain
about any matter, and avow it as a base on which
they are to build a system of practice, they seldom
quite believe in it. If they smell a rat about the
precincts of a cherished institution, they will always
stop their noses to it if they can.

Samuel Butler, 'Erewhon', chapter XVIII

1

A Loss of Direction

> Penal 'treatments', as we significantly describe them,
> do not have any reformative effect. . . . The dilemma
> is that a considerable investment has been made in
> various measures and services. . . . Are these services
> simply to be abandoned on the basis of the
> accumulated research evidence? Will this challenge
> evoke a response . . . by the invention of new
> approaches and new methods? (Croft 1978)

It is not difficult to produce evidence of confusion and
unease among those social workers in the probation and
after-care service and the local authority social services
departments whose task is to provide a social work service
linked to the criminal justice system. Recent publications
convey even in their titles a sense of change and
uncertainty — *Probation: a Changing Service* (Haxby
1978), or *Pressures and Change in the Probation Service*
(King 1979). Even the Home Office's recruitment pamphlet
no longer calls itself 'The probation and after-care service
as a career', but 'The probation and after-care service in a
changing society'. Walker and Beaumont (1981) are more
explicit in their recent book, which begins with a chapter
entitled simply 'Something's wrong'. Any attempt to
respond to this sense of uncertainty and loss of direction
has to start by trying to understand what has been
happening over the last ten years to our ideas about social
work with offenders, and how such work might develop in
the future.

To dispel any feeling that our current uncertainty about

the future of social work with offenders is simply another example of social workers' notorious propensity for navel-gazing, it is instructive to compare the present predicament with the position only a few years ago, well within the professional lifetimes of many still active in this field. Willis has pointed to a movement, over the last twenty or thirty years, from 'therapeutic optimism' to 'correctional nihilism' (Willis 1981) and my own career caught the tail-end of the sixties' optimistic explosion of social work effort in the criminal justice field. In those days, the perfectibility of man seemed more immediately achievable than now, and the general sense that society was open to change gave a new confidence to anyone with a stake in social engineering. The 'sixties feeling' of emancipation and enhanced possibilities, with its short-lived and unstable basis in the refusal of affluent educated youth to conform without question, has been amply documented by any number of commentators. Pearson (1975) particularly relates it to the social work field and to the emergence of a radical critique of social work activities. But before the radical critique (of which more later) really began to bite, social work in the late sixties and early seventies reflected the optimism of the times, in which good intentions, faith and commitment were more important than tedious detail.

At the end of the sixties, social workers could look forward with confidence and enthusiasm: the Seebohm Committee had accepted the arguments of many leaders in the profession for a unified social work department in every local authority (Hall 1976), offering generic social work to a wider range of clients than ever before, while the juvenile courts were preparing for a new Children and Young Persons Act which appeared substantially to restrict their decision-making powers in favour of a reliance on the expert judgement of social workers. Probation orders, described by Radzinowicz (1958) as 'the most significant contribution made by this country to the new penological theory and practice', were being used more and more by the courts. Social work in general, and social work with offenders in particular, seemed likely to grow in influence and importance and to become increasingly confident and assertive about its contribution to criminal justice.

In those days, probation officers trained on books like Monger's *Casework in Probation* (1964) and Foren and Bailey's *Authority in Social Casework* (1968), and absorbed an image of a criminal justice system moving rapidly towards an enlightened faith in rehabilitation. Offenders would be influenced by understanding, support and the esoteric skills of casework into becoming good conforming citizens. Any worries about imposing rehabilitation on clients who were not obviously voluntary were fairly easily calmed: after all, it was better than prison or other pointless non-rehabilitative punishments. Any reluctance on the part of an offender to follow the programme laid down by society through the court showed his failure to appreciate his real interests, and was itself part of his problem, confirming his need for help. In the long run, his interests and those of society coincided, enabling the social worker to serve both without excessive dissonance. Any apparent contradiction between the client's view of what was best for him and society's view could be resolved by reference to his client status: social work clients were expected to lack insight, which is why they needed social workers. What others might see as a conflict of aims, or even interests, between individuals and groups in society could be redefined as an intra-psychic conflict within the client, to be resolved by increasing his understanding of himself. This comforting circularity was confirmed by cases in the literature, such as Dr Hunt's Borstal boy, apparently sent there on his probation officer's advice, who writes to thank the officer: 'Really what I needed when I was little was a good hiding but I always knew I would not get one, but this is just as good as one although it has taken a long time to bring me to my senses' (Hunt 1964). Several authorities suggested that offending, particularly by young people, expressed an unconscious need for authority and control: they unwittingly offended in order to get caught and be controlled. This meant that they were virtually voluntary clients anyway, except that they didn't know it.

Although there may be a few cases which this kind of explanation will fit, it will hardly pass muster as a general theory of delinquency; however, it was a convenient and comforting view for social workers who did not want to see themselves as controlling or coercive, but as part of a humane profession which valued human dignity and self-determination, and preferred to work on the basis of a voluntary therapeutic relationship. Case committees, in which probation officers discussed their work with magistrates, were on the whole occasions of benign consensus where officers deferred to the status of magistrates and magistrates to the expertise of officers. Only the covert cynicism of the occasional unrehabilitated justices' clerk marred the harmonious atmosphere. Probation officers had brought off the apparently impossible trick of being congratulated by Authority for helping offenders. Again Radzinowicz (1958) provides a neat summary: 'Probation is fundamentally a form of social service preventing further crime by a readjustment of the culprit.' Whatever reservations might be felt by young social scientists trained to ask awkward questions, or by an older generation of probation officers who saw their work as common sense rather than therapy, the public face of social work with offenders was clearly to be identified with 'rehabilitation through casework'.

During the seventies, a number of developments contributed to the erosion of this comfortable consensus. For simplicity, these can perhaps be summarised as affecting the probation service in three main ways. First, there were changes in probation's social mandate: the job expected of the service by society became subtly different. Secondly, there were developments in the empirical base of the service's work which tended to question its commitment to rehabilitation. Thirdly, and partly in response to the first two changes, officers' views of their own work began to change, and a larger and more diverse service became an arena for discreet conflict between very different ideologies and perceptions. Meanwhile, similar processes were affecting social work with juvenile offenders in the new local authority social services departments, further complicated by the size of the agencies, the diversity of their tasks and the emergence of other priorities following child abuse scandals (DHSS 1974).

Taking the social mandate first, perhaps the most obvious change taking place during the seventies was the rapid extension of the probation service's duties into more and more areas of the penal system. 'Prison welfare' and after-care had already been added, but in 1970 probation orders made by courts, with the defendant's consent, still constituted 63 per cent of the service's caseload. Ten years later they were 28 per cent (Home Office 1981a), and they had also fallen in absolute numbers and as a proportion of those sentenced. In other words the probation order itself, traditionally the core of the service's work and the source of the title probation officer, played a decreasing role both in the sentencing practice of the courts and in the workload of the service. Paradoxically, this decline does not seem to be attributable to a high social inquiry workload, as many officers felt at the time; David Haxby (1978) has amply demonstrated that the figures do not support such a view. Instead, the most likely explanation seems to be an increased selectivity by officers in 'recommending' probation only for those judged to be amenable to casework, combined with a willingness on the part of sentencers to follow their advice. The space vacated in officers' workloads by the missing probation orders was taken up mainly by increases in statutory after-care and other forms of supervision which did not require the client's consent. In 1980 these constituted 34 per cent of the service's caseload.

New duties were created by the 1972 Criminal Justice Act as part of a package of measures designed to ease the pressure on the overcrowded prison system. Although, in retrospect, their success has been limited, they had a considerable effect within the probation service through the introduction of the community service order, a new sentence to be supervised by the probation service in the community but in which social work was not the main emphasis. The service's function was to be supervisory, ensuring the satisfactory completion of the required number of hours of unpaid labour. The police and the prison service had been seriously considered as potential supervisory agencies before the choice finally settled on the probation service (Pease and McWilliams 1980) and whatever the virtues of this decision, the effects on the Service are still being worked through (Vanstone and Raynor 1981).

From being an outpost of social work within a penal and judicial system whose basic priorities were very different, the probation service was becoming integrated at all levels into the day-to-day operation of that system. With community service it acquired a new sentence to administer which was intended to play a major part in diverting minor offenders from unnecessary custodial punishment. It had also become intimately linked to the actual process of custodial punishment, preparing reports on offenders before they went into custody, providing welfare services within the institutions and exercising compulsory supervision when they came out. Probation officers had thoroughly penetrated the judicial and penal systems and could hardly expect to be unchanged themselves. Increasingly their role of 'readjusting the culprit' seemed more important than the element of 'social service'.

Perhaps the clearest indication of the changing role envisaged for the probation service by penal policymakers came in 1974, with the publication of a report on young adult offenders (the 'Younger Report': Advisory Council on the Penal System 1974). I have already described how earlier theorists of probation were able to gloss over the question of consent to an imposed therapeutic relationship by hypothesising that at some 'deeper' level of motivation the client really wanted what was being offered, and any surface unwillingness or indifference could be attributed to lack of insight. The Younger Report had a simpler approach to the question of consent. In advocating its proposed 'supervision and control' order — a form of supervision in the community involving compulsory powers far beyond those of a probation order — the report argues:

> A statutory requirement of consent to a supervision and control order would not be appropriate, since it is intended that the order should permit the imposition of types of control to which it would be unrealistic to expect the offender to give genuine consent at the outset of the order. It is of course true that, if the order is to be effective, there must be a measure of acquiescence on the offender's part.

This acquiescence was to be secured by the exercise of social work skills. The image of social work which pervades the Younger Report and similar documents is of a set of methods and techniques which can persuade, seduce or compel people into conformity with authoritative views of how they should behave. In this process of 'readjusting the culprit' by compulsory persuasion, the client's own wishes, feelings and interpretations of the world are bound to have only a secondary importance, and the distinction between consent and coercion is blurred. The usefulness of social work to the State is as a means of producing acquiescence in those subject to various kinds of penal measure, and the client's own view of the situation is a side-issue for social workers to talk their way skilfully around.

Many probation officers were uneasy about what

seemed to be the emerging trend. The *Probation Journal* carried articles arguing that 'probation officers find themselves obviously participating in the state's methods of social control . . . the probation officer continuously supports this system of class law' (Beaumont 1976). Others asked: 'Can we win the struggle to retain our caring function against all the odds which now assail it?' (Chapman 1977) or argued that 'the Service must decide whether it wants essentially to help or control' (Jarman 1974). Discussions of this kind have continued ever since, with some officers anxious about becoming 'screws on wheels' while others argue that, like it or not, the probation service is part of the system of crime control and must order its attitudes and priorities accordingly. The details of these arguments need not concern us here, and are discussed more fully later. The essential point is that policy-makers expected the probation service to play a wider and more controlling role in the penal system, and controversy grew within the service itself between supporters and opponents of this trend. Meanwhile the courts continued to make fewer and fewer probation orders, suggesting at least that the traditional product was losing some of its appeal. Some commentators saw greater integration with the penal system as providing the best protection against possible marginality or irrelevance; for instance, the director of NACRO wrote a paper advocating a merger between the probation and prison services (Hinton 1976) in recognition of their overlapping functions. Others felt that the service's separation and distinctiveness was a necessary protection against becoming a token gesture towards 'welfare' within a basically punitive system.

This threat of incorporation or co-option is well illustrated by the anarchist Victor Serge in his account of his sentence in a French prison during the Great War. Here is his view of the function of prison chaplains and almoners:

The whole ambiguous duplicity of the chaplain's calling was apparent to me here, as was the whole revolting sham of his function. Even more revolting because the man was sincere and kind, resigned to his sacerdotal calling with that inner toughness which a social conscience gives to the intelligent bourgeois. The guillotine, doubtless, is not Christian. But the guillotine is necessary to the Christians. The death of Pierre Durand, at a predetermined hour, 'by verdict of law' . . . is a horrible thing. But the justice that commands that death is sacred. The pastor's duty is to sympathise with Pierre Durand's final anguish. His 'social' duty is to make sure the guillotine functions properly. Christian compassion plays its part, as does the oiling of the blade. (Serge 1969)

In addition to the stresses and pressures arising from changes in the penal system itself, the probation service during the seventies gradually became subject to a second set of pressures or sources of uneasiness. The claim to 'readjust the culprit', or treat offenders in such a way as to reduce their tendency to offend, came gradually to look increasingly precarious. The classic texts of correctional casework, like most social work literature of their time, included little evidence of the effectiveness of the methods they described except in the form of case histories and anecdotes. Foren and Bailey (1968) to their credit included an appendix on research, but it is not central to their argument and they seem mainly to have relied on a confident consensus within the social work profession that their methods were almost self-evidently effective, although evidence already existed to question this belief.

Two influential early studies can serve as examples. The Cambridge Somerville Youth Study (Powers and Witmer 1951) and the 'Vocational High' experiment (Meyer, Borgatta and Jones 1965) attempted to assess the effectiveness of social work and counselling services, with rather discouraging results. In the first of these, begun as early as 1937, a group of 325 boys aged from six to ten and judged to be delinquent or 'pre-delinquent' were assigned to social workers over an eight-year period with the objective of reducing their delinquency as measured by court appearances. An equal number of similar boys were randomly assigned to an untreated 'control' group. When outcomes were compared 96 of the experimentals had appeared for 264 offences, whereas 92 controls had appeared for 218 offences. Similarly in the Vocational High experiment, a group of high-school girls identified as potential problems were involved in an individual and group counselling programme. Compared to a similar control group, they showed only minimal and insignificant differences on a variety of measures. The foreword to the report of this study includes the significant question: 'Is social work on the wrong track?'

A number of other studies, mainly in America, appeared to question the efficacy of social workers' methods in achieving their stated goals and an increasing amount of research in the criminological and penological fields pointed almost unanimously to the unreliability of rehabilitation programmes, whether based on counselling, variations in institutional regimes, longer or shorter sentences or whatever. Comprehensive reviews undertaken by Martinson and his colleagues in America and by Brody for the Home Office Research Unit in Britain echo each other's conclusions (Lipton, Martinson and Wilks 1975; Brody 1976): 'We have very little reason to hope that we have in fact found a sure way of reducing recidivism through rehabilitation' (Martinson 1974). Brody frames it more cautiously but conveys the same message: 'Any assumption that different sentences, institutions or 'treatments' are affecting offenders in significantly different ways needs to be carefully reappraised.'

The Home Office itself was becoming involved in an ambitious programme of research into the British criminal justice system, and into the probation service in particular.

A few years after the optimistic Cambridge study of the results of probation (Radzinowicz 1958) Hammond of the Home Office Research Unit carried out an elaborate reconviction study of defendants receiving the full range of different sentences and found that for offenders of similar ages with comparable records, probation was on the whole about as likely as other sentences to lead to reconviction. This research attracted surprisingly little attention, perhaps because its results were tucked away in an appendix to a Home Office sentencing guide for magistrates and judges (Home Office 1969). Its comparisons between offenders receiving different sentences are based on matching by a limited range of criteria and pay no attention to the circumstances of offenders or any particular social or personal difficulties at the time when sentences were passed, but nevertheless it held little encouragement for those who regarded effective rehabilitation as the main justification for probation orders.

Another series of studies concentrated on the probation order itself, and included a sophisticated experiment in Intensive Matched Probation and After-Care Treatment (IMPACT) designed to test the hypothesis that more intensive 'treatment' applied by officers with lower caseloads would have better results. It is easy to imagine the claims for higher staffing and greater resources which would have followed a positive result. In the event, however, the comparison of reconviction rates between the low intensive caseloads and the controls given 'normal' supervision showed no significant difference in outcome. (In this it resembled much, but not all, research into the effectiveness of reduced caseloads — see for instance Adams 1967). Worse, the slight differences in reconviction that could be identified were in favour of the control group. The reaction of the probation service was odd. Although the early stages of the experiment had been greeted with some enthusiasm since they created opportunities for flexible and innovative work in the experimental teams, the final report (Folkard, Smith and Smith 1976) was greeted with a deafening silence and one has to look hard for any references to it in the professional literature. A further study of environmental social work by probation officers (Davies 1974) produced similarly discouraging results.

Social work generally is notorious for the slow penetration of research findings into actual practice, and several studies have shown that in reality social workers do not read or use much research. Some writers interpret this as a defensive device to avoid encountering evidence of ineffectiveness (Fischer 1976). However, some probation officers did read the research and found themselves in an odd position, continuing to produce traditional reports for courts which argued that a probation order offered the best prospect of influencing an offender away from crime, while knowing how hard it would be to substantiate such a claim. Innovation in methods (groupwork, family therapy, Heimler social functioning scales) and facilities (day centres, literacy schemes, accommodation schemes) flourished, but in a rather uncritical context. Few basic grade officers and fewer of their managers had the kind of skills in evaluative research which would have enabled a reliable separation of the promising innovations from the others, and so patterns of practice depended largely on the enthusiasm of individual practitioners and the support or otherwise of management. At the same time the expansion of the service, its regrouping by local government reform into larger units and the development of more extensive management hierarchies led to a greater insistence on accountability to and control by management. This control was often of a bureaucratic kind, concerned more with record-keeping and the prompt submission of statistics than with measuring or developing the effectiveness of services (Burnham 1981).

Meanwhile outside the probation service the local authority social workers dealing mainly with the younger juvenile offenders were affected by many of the same pressures, compounded by their unfamiliarity with their new role in the courts and by a conflict with other urgent duties. The fine hopes expressed in the White Paper *Children in Trouble* (Home Office 1968) had been watered down somewhat in the piecemeal implementation of the Children and Young Persons Act 1969, and the social workers charged with putting them into practice were an obvious target for criticism in courts which were used to dealing with probation officers. A complex interaction developed between an increasing 'moral panic' about juvenile crime and an identification of the 1969 Act (and the social workers who implemented it) as being somehow responsible for a new permissiveness and softness in dealing with 'young thugs'. Newspapers carried stories of bewildered magistrates unable to send offenders into custody because they were forced instead to make 'care orders' which gave social workers the power to send the delinquent child straight home again. Much of this was exaggerated or straightforwardly untrue, but when Rhodes Boyson made his much-quoted remark that 'social workers are part of the trouble with Britain', he had their involvement with juvenile justice in mind.

The real story of the 1969 Act is now known. Behind the media distortions and the posturing of politicians, juvenile justice in the seventies saw a massive increase in the use of custodial sentences for offenders aged from 14 to 17. This increase was both absolute and proportional as a share of total sentences. In other words, the use of custodial punishment increased far faster than the overall increase in juvenile crime, which was in any case much exaggerated. The practical effects of the Act on sentencing were little short of a disaster. Taking just the use of detention centres as an example, 5,800 offenders under 17 were sent to them in 1980, as compared to 1,800 in 1969, while the use of supervision in the community declined from nearly 20,000 probation orders on juveniles in 1969 to less than 16,500 supervision orders in 1980. Some studies have suggested that social workers have unintentionally contributed to this trend, partly by recommending custodial sentences on 'treatment' grounds and partly through the use of intermediate treatment groups as a voluntary resource, reducing their credibility as an alternative to custody (Thorpe, Smith, Green and Paley 1980).

It is against this background that we have to react to hints like the quotation from Croft which began this chapter by raising the question of whether social work services for offenders can be justified at all. Consequently the discussion so far has concentrated on negatives, and many of the issues raised will be re-examined in a different way later. However, the central question cannot be evaded. Social work with offenders is in a state of some confusion and uncertainty in which neither the goals nor the methods of the past three decades can be defended with conviction. Yet those of us who continue to be connected with this field also see a contrasting picture of commitment, intelligent innovation, constructive criticism and creative practice which make this an exciting time to be involved in the work. Courts and clients continue to use the probation service and the local authority services and often demonstrate considerable trust and confidence in their social workers and probation officers. Some offenders make great efforts to change their lives, and some succeed. Clearly social work still has a role to play in the criminal justice system, but what role? How should it be played? To begin to sketch some possible answers requires an initial excursion into wider fields of social work and social science.

2

Labels, Structures and Results: Three Critiques of Social Work

The loss of a sense of direction in social work with offenders is partly a problem of the criminal justice system, which has begun to lose faith in its capacity to influence offenders away from crime. However, it should not be seen simply as a problem for the penologists. Social workers who work with offenders share a common training, common methods and a largely common professional identity with other kinds of social worker, and their problems are closely connected with doubts and uncertainties affecting the whole enterprise of social work. Seldom has any profession experienced such a barrage of hostility and criticism as have social workers in the last decade, and to understand the situation of social work in criminal justice we must re-examine some of these criticisms and the profession's possible responses to them.

Any future historian of social work is likely to recognise three powerful and more or less distinct currents in the criticisms levelled against the profession in recent years. Ironically, they flow from sources which have very little in common and embody very different approaches to social science. They can for simplicity be identified as the interactionist critique, the structural critique and the empirical critique. We need to consider briefly the main characteristics of each.

REIFICATION AND THE POWER OF LABELS

The interactionist critique of social work, and of most activities directed towards reducing or correcting social problems, is based on the interest developed by sociologists and criminologists of the sixties in the attribution and maintenance of deviant identities, or 'labelling'. Starting from a position similar to that advanced in G. H. Mead's account of the development of identity (Mead 1934), early 'labelling' theorists such as Howard Becker and Edwin Lemert argued that what was distinctive and interesting about offenders (for instance) was not the presumed peculiarities which set them apart from other people, but rather the process by which they became set apart and deemed peculiar (Becker 1963; Lemert 1967). Despite differences of detail most sociologists of deviance who could be regarded as taking an interactionist approach would share certain basic positions. For instance, they would argue that social experience does not have inherent meaning, but has meanings conferred on it by actors through a process of interpretation, which is itself socially structured through the categories we have learned to use to interpret our experience. If we apply this to our experience of ourselves (in other words our sense of identity) and our interpretation of who someone else is, we would expect to find that identities are socially constructed over a period of time, and that our picture of ourselves and others is created and confirmed in and by social interactions. Our expectations of ourselves and others are influenced by our perception of the roles involved in a given social situation. This becomes particularly relevant to the position of people regarded as deviant when deviant status can be seen as an attribute of particular social roles, and it is then important to consider how an individual comes to occupy such a role.

The characteristic and striking argument of interactionists, which has led to their being grouped together as 'labelling' theorists, is that deviant social roles can be conferred on people in a signifying or labelling process which signals both to the labelled person and to the social audience that henceforth he or she is to be treated in a way which accords with the conferred role. The theme is familiar from proverbs ('give a dog a bad name') or literature (as in Jean Genet's youthful embracing of the offered identity of thief (Sartre 1952)), but its effect on criminology was to direct attention away from 'What sort of people become criminals?' (or mentally ill, homosexual or whatever) onto questions about how it happens, what perceptions and processes are involved, and what consequences of secondary deviation flow from the reaction of others. It is argued that in the right circumstances a deviant label, particularly if authoritatively applied to a relatively powerless person, can change personality or behaviour through a feedback process in which social situations influence self-perception and encourage the development of a deviant self-image.

A basic 'labelling' account of socialisation into deviant roles can be conveniently presented diagrammatically in flow-chart form (figure 1). This illustrates characteristic interactionist interest in feedback processes, vicious spirals and self-fulfilling prophecies.

Interactionists have been criticised for failing to provide a complete theory of deviance, though they claim in their own defence that they never purported to do so (Becker 1973). Their lack of interest in the perceived primary deviations which start the process, and their tendency to assume a certain passivity in the face of labelling processes, are perhaps necessary features of their deliberate concentration on what had hitherto been neglected, and certainly they threw a new light on a wide range of signifying processes from juvenile court proceedings (e.g. Cicourel 1968) to psychiatric diagnosis (e.g. Scheff 1966). The particular impact of this perspective on social work arises from its interest in how particular behaviours or particular people come to be identified as 'problems', or

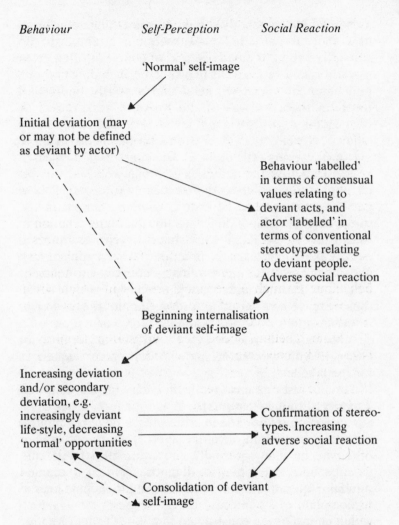

Figure 1   A 'labelling' model of socialisation into deviant roles

'A small initial deviation which is within the range of high probability may develop into a deviation of a very low probability indeed' (Wilkins 1964).

The dotted lines represent a possible self-labelling process, in which the subject provides his own adverse reaction, having learned to stereotype his own behaviour and regard it as deviant.

as 'something somebody should do something about', and
how they are affected by subsequent attempts to do
something about them. This task, of course, is often given
to various kinds of experts in problems, including doctors,
policemen or social workers, and an early interest of
labelling theorists was in the possible aggravation or
consolidation of problems ('deviancy amplification') as a
result of the efforts of professional problem-correctors.

Ironically, very little of the classic interactionist research
concentrated on the activities of social workers, and yet
its impact on social work has been profound. This is
partly because it has become a routine element in the
social science educational background shared by many
recent recruits to social work, but it also arises from the
close links which exist in practice between social work
and other areas such as psychiatry and law-enforcement
which the interactionists studied zealously. Particularly in
these areas they raised questions about the powerful
labelling activities of professionals, often carried out on a
slender basis of evidence, with little consideration of
alternative interpretations and with serious consequences
for the labelled persons.

To take just one example from each of these fields, an
American study of psychiatric diagnosis found that when
a number of pseudopatients were presented at psychiatric
hospitals complaining of a few stereotyped symptoms but
otherwise behaving normally, they were all detained and
given specific psychiatric diagnoses which remained
officially operative even when the pseudopatients ceased
to complain of symptoms. Their 'wellness' was invisible
within an institution constructed to follow the authoritative
opinions of doctors. The research quotes examples of the
pseudopatients' true life histories being solemnly entered
in case records as confirmatory evidence of disorder. The
taking of research notes appeared in the files as 'patient
engages in writing behaviour', and when the pseudopatients were eventually judged safe to release this was
typically done under the diagnostic label 'schizophrenia

in remission' (Rosenhan 1973). A follow-up experiment warned hospitals that pseudopatients were being sent and then sent none, with the result that substantial numbers of real patients were turned away as fakes.

This neatly illustrates some worrying features of diagnosis which have obvious parallels in the social work field. Diagnostic statements by social workers or psychiatrists aspire to be explanations of behaviour, but often involve the kind of circularity illustrated in Rosenhan's experiment. Many apparent diagnoses in social work (e.g. 'inadequate recidivist') are in reality no more than shorthand descriptions of behaviour ('he has had difficulties in coping with life and has often committed offences'). But when they pose simultaneously as *explanations* of behaviour ('he continues to offend *because* he is an inadequate recidivist') they create an illusion of understanding and sometimes a self-confirming impression of predictability ('and so he will keep on offending, so what can we do?'). Once diagnosed, there is a danger of treating the subject as a predictable object and his behaviour as a causally determined outcome of his diagnosed condition rather than something to be explained (like our own behaviour and that of 'normal' people) by reference to reasons, choices and other considerations which do not arise in objects. This is how we can notice the patient 'engaging in writing behaviour' without the slightest interest in what he may be writing, except perhaps as a symptom. We have labelled him in such a way that we can experience him as a thing rather than as a person like ourselves. This reification can them become a self-confirming process which invalidates claims by the client or patient for restoration of normal identity — indeed, protests can be taken as confirmation of deviant status. The perils of wielding the symbolic power of diagnosis are difficult to reconcile with traditional social work values of respect for persons.

Another field close to social work in which the interactionists have been busy is that of law enforcement, particularly where legal measures are used as part of an intended preventive response to social problems. Young's study of drug-takers in London in the sixties shows some typical features of interaction between 'problem' groups and official control agents. In this case the main characters are young people using prohibited soft drugs for hedonistic recreation, and the local police (Young 1971).

Young documents a process whereby young drug-users, mostly with normal jobs and fairly conventional values, were seen by the police as a serious threat to themselves and others, who needed to be energetically prevented and rescued 'for their own good'. He suggests that police expectations of drug problems were based largely on stereotypes of 'dope fiends' derived from American opiate-addicts, and stresses that the police were, on the whole, well meaning and benevolent, wanting to save the drug-takers from themselves. Police attention was interpreted by its objects as persecution, leading to greater group solidarity, a sense of more 'common ground' with each other and less with outsiders, the beginnings of an alternative subculture and a developing atmosphere of isolation, secrecy and paranoia. The police were stereo-typed in their turn as oppressive 'pigs', and libertarian or radical ideologies provided a rationale for personal stances of opposition. Drug use continued at a higher level of risk and at higher prices, which allowed higher profit margins and attracted the attention of professional criminals. These increasingly figured in the commercial supply of drugs which had originally been distributed between friends and acquaintances on a largely non-profit-making basis. Professional dealers had an interest in creating addicts, and began to harden the drug market. In this way, argues Young, a criminalised subculture developed partly in response to official actions which were based on an incorrect assumption that it existed from the beginning. A social control effort based on fundamentally benevolent aims but defective understanding had contributed to a greatly increased polarization of attitude between police and a section of the public, and had been instrumental in creating the very situation it set out to prevent.

The message of this kind of study for social workers is all too clear. Social workers give attention to people on the basis of problems they are believed to have, and the danger of amplifying or imputing problems is obvious. Client status itself can be seen as implying inadequacy. Jordan has suggested that modern social work agencies can structure the client role in particularly demeaning and unhelpful ways:

> From now on, you get by only by virtue of your social problems. You qualify for money by your children being in danger of reception into care, for accommodation by being evicted and homeless, for health care by being chronic and incurable, for education by being backward or beyond control. From now on you must never be entitled, always desperate; never angry, always threatening; never confused, always mental; never upset, always suicidal. Present yourself as in a material sort of crisis, but also in a personal kind of mess, about to break-up or break-down or (if in Scotland) likely to become a heavier expense to the council on another occasion if you remain unassisted. (Jordan 1975)

Although this is presented as the kind of 'script' covertly written for clients by social services departments and Scottish social work departments, it provides no grounds for smugness in probation. After all, it is by no means self-evident that the best way to shake off a criminal identity is to be required to report regularly for two or three years to a special kind of official who deals with criminals.

SOCIAL WORK AND SOCIAL STRUCTURE

The second major source of social scientists' criticisms of

social work has been their consideration of the social
functions of social work in a stratified society where
power and wealth are unevenly distributed. It is suggested
that social workers serve the interests of the powerful,
rather than the powerless who constitute their clientele.
They provide only palliatives for their clients' problems,
moderating their discontent and providing what is
fundamentally a token form of 'welfare'. This both
substitutes for and helps to avoid the genuine redistribution
of power and resources which, it is argued, would serve
clients' interests better. At the very least, social workers
serve as state functionaries in a Welfare State which has
functions other than the provision of welfare (such as the
maintenance of social stability, existing patterns of
privilege and corresponding deprivation). Social workers
themselves, it is suggested, have been ill equipped to
recognise this. As C. Wright Mills put it as long ago as
1943:

> Present institutions train several kinds of people —
> such as judges and social workers — to think in
> terms of 'situations'. Their activities are set within
> the existing norms of society: in their professional
> work they tend to have an occupationally trained
> incapacity to rise above 'cases'. It is in part through
> such concepts and methods as the 'case approach'
> that social pathologists have been intellectually tied
> to social work with its occupational position and
> political limitations. (Mills 1943)

The argument is that as long as social workers
uncritically take for granted a consensus viewpoint which
explains the deprivation of their clients as a consequence
of individual deficiencies, they are likely to adopt an
individualistic case-by-case approach both to understanding
and to resolving problems which are in fact shared by, or
imposed collectively upon, large numbers of people. A
preference for individualistic psychological diagnosis can

help to disguise the social dimensions of problems, and an ideology of treatment 'for the client's own good' can often provide a rhetorical screen to disguise coercion or overtly controlling practices. Perhaps this deceives social workers more effectively than it deceives their clients. Handler, in his study of children's departments in London before the Seebohm reforms (Handler 1973), gives accounts of social workers' decisions to precipitate the eviction of families by not using discretionary powers under the 1963 Children and Young Persons Act to meet rent arrears. These decisions, which appear on face value to have something to do with maintaining social controls within the rented housing market, tended to be justified in terms of the supposed therapeutic needs of clients — 'they need to be helped to face reality'. This mystification then served to protect social workers against awareness of conflict between their controlling or coercive functions and their traditional principles of 'acceptance' and 'self-determination'.

This kind of criticism now seems curiously dated, and much of it reflects a social work rather different from current practice. Wootton, writing 25 years ago, could effectively attack the basis of social work theory by arguing against the doctrines of psychoanalysis, confident that the same arguments would do for both occupations (Wootton 1959). Social workers are now less dominated by psychoanalytic thinking, but are they any clearer about their place in a divided and unequal society?

In 1972 a group of Marxist, socialist and libertarian social workers loosely organised around the magazine *Case Con* produced a statement of aims which included this analysis of the social work role:

> We oppose the use of social workers as tranquillisers and agents of social control, who thereby help to buttress the present system. We support the attempts of social workers to engage in community action and encourage the activities of grass-roots organisations such as claimants' unions and tenants' associations.

We oppose the authoritarian organisation of
training courses and a curriculum biased solely
towards the location of problems in individual
pathology, with a consequent emphasis on the
casework solution. (Case Con Collective 1971)

Here we see again the equation between a concern for
individual psychologistic accounts of problems and
uncritical support for a repressive consensus in a State
which promotes inequality. The only viable stance for a
social worker seems to be opposition. Similarly, the
introduction to an influential collection of readings on
radical social work (Bailey and Brake 1975) presents the
capitalist State (with all its apparatus of armies, police and
welfare agencies) as acting consistently to maintain the
working class in subjection. The Welfare State is seen as
'sustaining rather than undermining the established
situation', and it exists simply in order to provide a pool of
healthy labour for capitalist industry. According to this
argument, social workers are expected to be cogs in a
state machine which is in the last analysis more concerned
with control and exploitation than with welfare. Such a
view leaves very little space for genuinely helpful social
work within State agencies.

Not all writers on radical social work offer this analysis
of the State, and the proper understanding of the social
worker's role in the State apparatus has become a
continuing debate. The view that everything the State
does, from policing to health care, works against working-
class interests has been criticised as 'left idealism' (e.g.
Lea and Young 1984). Other writers have stressed the
relative autonomy of a State which they see as reflecting
the current balance of conflicting class interests and not
necessarily directly serving any single class all the time
(e.g. Corrigan and Leonard 1978). On this view, welfare
services reflect a genuine and useful advance rather than
a misleading palliative, but because of their provision by a
State which reflects contradictory interests they are

subject to particular kinds of distortion. For instance they may be subject to economic erosion when some other part of the State's concerns demands resources; they may tend to define problems ideologically, by attributing them to individual malfunction rather than to the uneven distribution of resources; they may provide services in a form which accentuates dependency and stigma; and they may find themselves drawn into a position where their primary function is to control potentially troublesome or demanding sections of the population rather than helping to meet their needs.

Peter Leonard, drawing both on interactionist theories and on arguments about social structure, suggests that social workers are typically invited to understand their role as re-integrating deviant individuals who are defined as problems by reference to a widely shared consensus about what is normal and socially 'healthy'. Clients are marginal and abnormal individuals needing to be re-socialised in their own interest as well as everyone else's. Arguing that this consensus image of society is a reassuring fiction, he suggests that many of the problems assigned to social work are better understood in terms of models which recognise the reality of conflicts of values and conflicts of interest between different groups (Leonard 1976). For instance, a pluralist analysis will emphasise differences and potential disputes between different sections of society and will stress the need to preserve patterns of adaptation, compromise and containment of conflict. The role of social workers and other welfare officials can then be seen in terms of advocacy and mediation, assisting in processes of mutual understanding and mutual adjustment. Alternatively, a conflict analysis of the relationship between different social groups will stress the exercise of power by some groups over others and the incompatible material interests arising from relationships of economic exploitation. Here the space for compromise is seen as limited and largely illusory. The social worker's role is either to exercise control over his clients on behalf of the system, or to adopt what Leonard calls an adversary role and fight back.

It is fair to point out, as Davies (1981) has done in another context, that questions about the goals and objectives of change and about whose interests the social worker serves arise mainly in respect of change-promoting tasks where the social worker's job is to influence (or persuade or compel) someone to alter behaviour which has been defined as a problem. He points out, realistically, that much social work is 'maintenance' work, concerned with supporting clients or meeting need of an ideologically uncontentious kind. Does arranging the delivery of meals-on-wheels require so much soul-searching about the function of social work in society? Perhaps not, unless we are concerned about the criteria for qualification, or the level of provision, or the social changes which have led to an elderly person's isolation, or the nature and sources of the dependency forced on most of our old people. Davies indeed implies that social workers only confuse and distress themselves with sociological speculation and should instead demonstrate 'a broad acceptance of the existing political and economic regime'. However, there are large areas of social work where this kind of opting out of political or moral debate is particularly difficult and inappropriate, and the probation service, with its implicit task of influencing its clients towards 'right' behaviour, is clearly one of these morally contentious areas. The problems posed by Leonard's analysis for the probation officer, with so few voluntary clients and carrying such a heavy weight of consensual expectations, are considerable.

This brief survey of structural criticisms of social work's function does scant justice to a large and varied literature, reflecting all varieties of Marxian and radical thought. Many themes have not even been touched on — for instance, the questioning of social workers' alleged concern to promote a 'normal' family life which facilitates sex-role stereotyping and the exploitation of women (e.g.

Wilson 1977). The literature of radical social work is stronger on theoretical analysis than on practical suggestions, but whatever its weaknesses as a developed guide to action, it encourages a cool reappraisal of much that social workers have traditionally taken for granted.

John Rex, in developing his conflict analysis of industrial societies and confronting the question of why there is not more overt and continuous conflict in them, developed the concept of the 'social system of the truce', in which ruling groups have had to make substantial and long-term concessions to the needs of subject groups (Rex 1961). The development of welfare institutions is seen as part of this 'system of the truce', and Rex argues that this can be regarded as qualitatively different from a system based on naked coercive domination. The 'truce' represents a relatively durable compromise or balance, inherently unstable yet often self-correcting as many groups have an interest in maintaining it (not least those who staff and operate the welfare services). Confusion and conflict about aims, objectives and values are endemic in the 'system of the truce', since it reflects the contradictions and conflicts of the society which has generated it, but the institutions themselves are relatively persistent rather than transitory. (They even show a fair degree of durability in the face of a Conservative Government far more hostile to welfare measures than most people would have expected at the time when Rex was writing.) Little thought has been given to the precise implications for social worker roles within such a system, but it is clear that they would be complex, often contradictory and subject to continuous reappraisal. They would lack the reassuring clarity and certainty which we sometimes seek by basing our practice on a priori theoretical stances. But how much clarity and certainty do we actually achieve in this way? The probation service during the early seventies developed its own radical faction, the NAPO Members' Action Group, which reflected many of the concerns of Case Con and elaborated its own position in a well-known

Working Document. This document discusses (over 16 pages) the social context, the history of social work, the role and function of the probation officer, various possibilities of progressive and socialist action within the probation service, management, training and trade unionism (NMAG 1976). What to do with the service's clients occupies one paragraph, which finds it necessary to remind us that 'it is clearly impossible to do the job conscientiously without involvement with the individual clients and their needs. Some clients can benefit from such support.' This uncontroversial statement is then qualified: 'The better social worker you are, the more you help the system — but there is no denying that there are casualties of the system needing and asking for help.' The dilemma is unresolved and the document offers little guidance for a radical social work practice.

Case Con itself was caught in the same trap, and later issues (before its demise in 1977) were largely devoted to trade union matters rather than to the radical reappraisal of professional practice which gave the earlier issues their distinctive originality and excitement. More recent radical social work texts (Corrigan and Leonard 1978, Brake and Bailey 1980) have made more resolute attempts to grasp the nettle by suggesting concrete examples of radical practice, but the main contribution of the radical critique is still to question the 'old' social work rather than to reconstruct it on any firmer base. Radical positions on social policy and reformist proposals for criminal justice have won support in the National Association of Probation Officers, now a registered trade union and the regular scene of battles between left and right, but the radical analysis has given less clear guidance for services to clients and I suspect that the average probation client might find it difficult to distinguish the radical officer from his conventional colleague. One of them may have shed his 'trained incapacity to rise above cases', but this may not always make much difference from the point of view of the 'case'.

THE EMPIRICAL CASE AGAINST TREATMENT

The third major source of criticism faced by social work during the last decade has been the accumulating evidence of research designed to test its effectiveness in producing positive change in clients' lives. The last chapter pointed out how research had largely failed to support probation's claim to 'prevent crime by a readjustment of the culprit'. In this, probation shows close links with other forms of social work which demonstrate similar results. Perhaps the best and most pointed summing up is provided by Joel Fischer, who conducted a thorough review of available research on the effectiveness of social casework and drew gloomy conclusions from the 17 studies which met his criteria of adequate experimental design (Fischer 1976). He makes his views clear: 'The bulk of practitioners in an entire profession appear, at worst, to be practicing in ways that are not helpful or even detrimental to their clients, and, at best, operating without a shred of empirical evidence validating their efforts.'

Fischer links this situation explicitly with social workers' tendency to identify their task with psychodynamic models of practice. This, he argues, leads to an overemphasis on insight, self-understanding and introspection at the expense of a focus on social functioning and environmental change. He criticises reliance on talk as the main therapeutic medium for all clients, and on theories which assist understanding rather than guiding action and are in any case notoriously difficult to test. These assessments echo Eysenck's comments on psychoanalysis (Eysenck 1966) and have about them something of the hard-headed researcher's impatience with intuitive and speculative procedures. Fischer's most scornful comments are reserved for caseworkers who 'became devoted to the "art" of practice at the expense of scientific input' (e.g. 'Casework is in essence an experience between two people' (Hollis 1968)).

Although Fischer and similar writers (e.g. Sutton 1979) can be criticised for taking too positivist an approach to an activity in which interpretation, perception and attitudes are vitally important, their concentration on technical issues of method (as opposed to 'casework principles' and vaguely stated good intentions) certainly helps to correct an imbalance in the literature. They remind us that social workers' activities are supposed to be purposeful and that we must have ways of finding out whether they achieve anything, not simply for reasons of accountability but because this is the only way practice can improve. There is little need to labour a point which has been so thoroughly stressed in recent writing, except to point out that any concern felt in the probation service about the results of evaluative research is more than matched in other branches of social work. Also it should be noted that Fischer's main concern is with psychodynamic casework, as typified by the idea of 'psychosocial therapy'. This no longer accurately describes either the whole of social work or the whole of the probation service.

Most evaluative studies of social work within the probation service and penal system have, as mentioned before, produced similarly discouraging results. If reduction in recidivism is taken as evidence of success most of the research provides no such evidence, suggesting either that the work done is ineffective or that the effectiveness of some practitioners may be cancelled out by the ineffectiveness and actual harmfulness of others. Social work is not on the whole a successful 'treatment of crime'. However, a few studies have considered the possibility of differential effects on different groups of offenders, and some of these present a slightly less gloomy picture which is worth exploring further. Two of the Home Office Research Unit studies are particularly interesting in this respect. Both attempt to compare outcomes of 'normal' social work services with more intensive contact, using control groups. One is in an institutional setting and the other in the community, but both make a serious attempt to identify which offenders benefited and which did not.

First, a project which produced a positive outcome where few expected to find one: *Social Work in Prison* (Shaw 1974). In this experiment, prisoners nearing the end of their sentences in one open and one closed prison were randomly assigned to experimental and control groups, and the experimental group was offered 'extended contact' (weekly sessions) with welfare officers (i.e. probation officers seconded to the prison). They could refuse, but few did. Controls had normal contact: that is, they could apply to see the welfare officer if they wished, but in practice had much less contact than the experimentals. While the main finding, that the experimentals were significantly less likely than the controls to be reconvicted in a two-year follow-up period, is itself important, there were also interesting results concerning the patterns of response to treatment. Some hypotheses (e.g. that 'anti-authority' prisoners would benefit less from intensive contact) were not confirmed, and in general there was little relationship between expectations of who would benefit and measured outcomes. The one measure which appeared to be significantly associated with an unusually high degree of benefit from the experimental programme was a measure of introversion derived from the Eysenck Personality Inventory. All introverts in the control group were reconvicted, and a majority of introverts in the experimental group were not. Extraverts (i.e. low scorers on introversion) showed no significant difference in reconviction between the two groups. As a group, the introverts were found to be less sociopathic than the extraverts, less involved in criminal subcultures and slightly more neurotic and anxious.

It is interesting to compare these findings with those of the final report of the Home Office's IMPACT experiment which compared the responses of probationers allocated to an experimental group, who received intensive supervision in reduced caseloads, with a control group given normal supervision. The main negative finding of this study has already been described; however, a search for interaction effects did yield some suggestive results. Those who did better in the control group than in the experimental group tended to be more extraverted, less neurotic and to have more previous convictions. The only clients who did slightly better under experimental treatment (although, with relatively small numbers, the difference did not reach statistical significance) were those who reported a high total of personal problems on the Mooney Problem Checklist completed by all participants in the experiment. Those reporting a low level of problems did significantly better under less intensive supervision. The difference was particularly marked for a group of clients who had medium or low Mooney problem totals and moderate or high 'criminal tendencies' (as judged by the officers completing the social enquiry report): these did noticeably better under less intensive supervision, achieving 25 per cent reconviction compared to 45 per cent for similar clients in the experimental group. For those with the opposite characteristics (high problem totals and low 'criminal tendencies'), there was a marked difference in favour of the experimental group, although again numbers were too small for the difference to be regarded as significant.

These results hardly support the Younger Committee's recommendation that offenders with considerable criminal involvement and little motivation to see supervision as helpful should be given more intensive compulsory supervision. In fact, there is a strong suggestion that more intensive supervision would make them worse. But what about those who seemed to benefit from the more intensive situation? It seems that these were people who were more aware of problems in their own lives, and more prepared to state and recognise them. The Mooney checklist also has the virtue of allowing people to state their own difficulties, rather than depending on someone else's assessment of them, however 'expert'.

Although one must be scrupulous about this group's failure to achieve statistical significance in its efforts to keep out of trouble, other studies have pointed in a similar direction. The PICO project (Pilot Intensive Counselling, reported by Adams 1961) offered intensive counselling to young adults in a vocational institute in California, and compared outcomes with an untreated control group. Both groups were further divided into those expected by the staff to be amenable to this kind of programme, and those judged unamenable. The typical 'amenable' subject was 'bright, verbal, anxious, aware of his difficulties and anxious to overcome them'. The 'amenables' in the experimental group eventually stayed out of trouble more successfully than those in the control group, whereas the treated 'unamenables' found themselves in more trouble than their counterparts in the control group.

To quote one more American example, the Community Treatment Project in California has produced a mass of material over the years in its attempts to assess the effectiveness of supervision in the community as against custodial methods of controlling young people involved in crime. From the outset, this project tried to distinguish between different types of offenders, using a typology and rating scales based on the concept of 'interpersonal maturity'. These involve five different maturity levels or 'I-levels' and various sub-types within them. The characteristics shown by people assigned to the lower maturity levels include a tendency to relate to others primarily in terms of their own needs, or to treat them as objects to be manipulated. Subjects at the higher levels show an awareness of other people's expectations, and attempt to live up to some internalised standards of conduct, with more evidence of anxiety or guilt. The majority of subjects at the higher levels also fall into a sub-type described as 'neurotic', and it is within this group that the largest and most consistent differences in reconviction in favour of the experimental group have been reported (Palmer 1974).

Findings like these can be interpreted in a number of ways, and any conclusions drawn are bound to be speculative, involving assumptions which the studies concerned were not specifically designed to test. However, if we treat them as straws in the wind, it is reasonable to comment on where they seem to be blowing. On the one hand, they provide some clues about the type of offender for whom conventional social work help seems to have produced some useful rehabilitative results. The methods used by the social workers, counsellors and probation officers involved seem broadly to have been based on attempts at understanding their clients as people, at trying to increase their understanding of themselves and their situations, and at exercising influence through various kinds of helping relationship. They did not aim at the impractical target of minute-by-minute control of clients' lives, which would perhaps be the only way to approach the coercive goal of guaranteed conformity to desired behaviour. The clients who benefited tend to attract labels such as 'neurotic' which suggest a degree of intrapersonal conflict, an awareness of a gap between what they do and what they want to do, or between the possibilities and the actualities of their lives. There are also indications that they tend to be people who are aware of their 'problems in living', and who realise or are close to realising that these problems have something to do with their own past and future choices. This adds up to a potential for change.

However, it is also clear that many of the offenders who are processed through the British criminal justice system would not easily fit this description. To regard social work within that system as a service mainly aimed at a small group of 'amenables' is to select the clients to fit the service provided, and the decrease from 1972 to 1978 in the use of probation orders may reflect an attempt by officers to select 'suitable' clients when writing their social inquiry reports. Such a process of 'matching' service and client is of course desirable but perhaps it went too far in the direction of making the client population fit into the particular forms of casework which officers preferred to practice, rather than adapting the service to suit a wider range of clients.

Read in this light, the studies have another interesting implication. If social workers' efforts with offenders are more likely to affect future offending when they fit in with clients' own perceptions of problems and of a need for help, this suggests that any progress made is likely to be in the direction of clients' own goals, or their own solutions to their own problems. Instead of 'helping' being seen primarily as a by-product of crime control, a kind of luxury or fringe benefit in a process directed primarily at reducing offences, perhaps crime control, if achieved at all in this kind of process, occurs primarily as a *by-product of helping.*

Some support for this view can be found even among the strongest opponents of 'rehabilitation'. For instance, the major American review of the effectiveness of correctional treatments points to some evidence that pre-release counselling in institutions can reduce recidivism 'if the counselling is directed towards the immediate problems confronted by those with criminal records who are attempting to live in the free community. These immediate problems include: housing, income, medical services, family services' (Lipton, Martinson and Wilks 1975). Similarly,

> to the degree that casework and individual counselling provided to offenders in the community is directed towards their immediate problems, it may be associated with reduction in recidivism rates. Unless

this counselling leads to solution of problems such as
housing, finances, jobs or illness which have high
priority for offenders, it is unlikely to have any impact
upon future criminal behaviour.

Such findings would support a decreasing emphasis on
psychodynamic casework preoccupied with a search for
underlying problems, which is likely to be useful only to a
minority of offenders, and an increased emphasis on
helping with problems actually faced by and identified by
clients. A later review of research on attempts to reduce
juvenile offending (Romig 1978) concludes that unfocused
and unspecific counselling methods, among which he
includes casework, tend to fail, where more favourable
results are attributable to approaches which have a clearer
focus on concrete and achievable goals in the clients'
everyday lives.

Findings of this kind are consistent with a variety of
evidence that social workers can work effectively when
their objectives reflect their clients' own perceptions of
problems and choices of goals. However, this poses
particular problems for social work services provided
within and through the criminal justice system. Social
workers may well perform more effectively in relation to
client-defined problems than in relation to an externally
defined problem like crime, which in any case seems so
complex in its aetiology and so much influenced by
situational factors outside the client's control that many
attempts at intervention are likely to have only marginal
effects. But social work services for offenders have
traditionally been seen as offering help not as an end in
itself but as a correctional technique, a means towards
rehabilitation or a 'treatment' for crime. It is easy to see
how this image of social work fits within a criminal justice
system which identifies its own function in correctional
terms. However, if effective helping is achieved in practice
in relation to client-defined problems, these problems

may not include offending. Clients may be, and often are, more concerned about other issues and more inclined to seek help with them. This kind of helping could be justified as serving correctional goals, and therefore constituting a legitimate concern of correctional criminal justice systems, only so long as we could sustain the belief that social work with offenders did, in practice, typically rehabilitate them. If we relegate rehabilitation to a secondary goal, achieved (if at all) as a by-product of services directed primarily towards helping, why should the criminal justice system contain and facilitate this kind of service?

The discredited concept of rehabilitation was certainly useful while it lasted. It provided a rationale for the humane goal of helping offenders and for persuading sentencers that helpful sentencing could serve their correctional purposes. The same arguments in reverse allowed probation officers and social workers to blur distinctions between helping and controlling, and to see their own activities as helpful even on those occasions when it might seem to their clients that they were simply administering the terms of a coercive sentence. The demise of rehabilitation leaves an enormous gap, and there is a temptation to ignore the evidence and 'muddle along'. In the long run, however, this is likely to prove a costly solution, commanding a heavy price in confusion and demoralisation.

Rehabilitation through casework, or 'preventing further crime by a readjustment of the culprit', will no longer serve as a credible unifying ideology for the probation service and the other social workers in the criminal justice system. A possible alternative candidate, which can more easily be defended against the criticisms outlined in this chapter, is some form of commitment to 'helping'. This might offer alternatives to reification by diagnostic labelling, to repressive 'treatment' on behalf of an oppressive society, or to the ineffective pursuit of rehabilitation. But under what conditions is 'helping' a relevant and acceptable goal for criminal justice? This is a complex and difficult question, and the next chapter examines some recent attempts within the probation service to develop alternative models of social work with offenders now that traditional models are increasingly hard to sustain.

3

Alternative Models of Probation Practice

In this part of the discussion, the emphasis must shift explicitly to recent debates within and around the probation service. This is not to discount the fact that a large proportion of social work with offenders is no longer the responsibility of that service, having been re-assigned to local authority social services departments by the 1969 Children and Young Persons Act, but simply to recognise that the major debates in this field have tended so far to take place in a probation context. This service remains, of course, the major employer of social workers who specialise in work with offenders, and is the only social work agency which depends primarily for its credibility and function on a special relationship with the criminal justice system. Local authorities have many other clients; probation officers draw all but a small proportion of their work from the criminal courts and penal institutions, and the remainder, although non-criminal, still flows from the court system through the involvement of civil courts in matrimonial disputes. Thus the problem of the role and function of social work in criminal justice is, for the probation service, not simply an issue of professional concern to a few practitioners but a question of survival, or at least of survival in a recognisable form.

The last few years in the probation service have been a time of uncertainty, creativity and debate. Practice has diversified into an unprecedented variety of programmes, styles and objectives from highly voluntaristic community projects to highly coercive and disciplined 'control units', each with articulate defenders and critics. In the absence of a strong 'official' consensus commanding widespread support, individuals have developed their own models of practice according to their own convictions and some managers discern a corresponding need for 'positive leadership' and more centralised control, without always being any clearer than their staff about the direction in which they should lead. Out of this interesting mixture some coherent perspectives have begun to crystallise, each with different implications for the future role and function of officers.

The main contending positions which have so far been articulated can be grouped under five headings:

1 *Separatism*, advocating the separation, both organisationally and in everyday practice, of the 'caring' and 'controlling' functions of the probation service;
2 *'Controlism'*, arguing for an explicit identification with punishment and control, in which the service's role will be to develop a wider range of punishments in the community;
3 *Radicalism*, attempting to articulate a practice consistent with a socialist or Marxist analysis of the function of the service in a capitalist society;
4 The *Sentenced to Social Work* approach, arguing for explicit supervision and surveillance of clients within limits set by the courts, with various kinds of help available in addition for those who are interested;
5 The *Non-Treatment* approach, substituting 'helping' objectives for 'rehabilitation' objectives and attempting to reconstruct a role for social work in the service without promising 'treatment for crime'.

These positions do not exhaust the range of views current or possible within the service. In particular, it is often argued that there is a 'silent majority' position, occupied by officers who simply get on with the job on a common-sense eclectic basis, supported by a healthy scepticism and a pragmatic intolerance of abstract ideas. There are also residual therapists who continue to see the job in terms of psychodynamic casework. However, this discussion is mainly concerned with what seem to be the main articulated contenders for the position of dominant ideology within the service, and pure pragmatism is increasingly difficult to sustain without some kind of agreed rationale to which practitioners can turn when called upon to account for their work or to make difficult decisions. Practitioners appeal to theoretical models for this kind of purpose even when they would see their everyday practice as primarily a common-sense process, and our concern here is with the models to which they might appeal in the absence of support for 'rehabilitation through casework'. Each model will be briefly examined to draw out some of its implications for the place of social work in the criminal justice system.

SEPARATING 'CARE' AND 'CONTROL'

The 'separatist' position has been developed mainly in two articles by Robert Harris (1977 and 1980). He argues that the expectation of courts and the public that probation officers will control offenders involves a fundamental clash with the social work objectives embodied in the skills and training of officers themselves. He recognises that arguments based on the efficacy of social work skills in preventing further offences are no longer convincing:

> The present system is ineffective in that compulsory supervision apparently makes no difference whatsoever to the likelihood of a client reoffending; it is also inappropriate for a trained social worker to have his avenues of referral controlled by a non-social worker magistrate; it is damaging to the many

defendants who are deprived of short-term assistance
by the fact that probation officers' functions do not
embrace their needs, no court order having been
made; it is damaging to the court, whose intentions
are liable to be thwarted by the ever-widening gap
between their expectations and those of the probation
officers to whose care the defendants are entrusted;
it is damaging to the officers who, by spending a high
proportion of their time fulfilling a function for which
they are not qualified, spend an accordingly smaller
proportion of time practising and developing their
professional skills. (Harris 1977)

In essence, this argument seems to be a restatement in
modern dress of the position against which Foren and
Bailey (1968) argued. Harris sees social work skills and the
meeting of deprived offenders' undoubted needs for help
as hampered and restricted by a framework of compulsory
contact under the orders of a court. Foren and Bailey's
argument that an element of coercion can enable social
work skills to be applied to the reform of offenders is
rightly seen as no longer convincing in the absence of
substantial evidence of successful reform by these means.
To this extent, Harris addresses the problems outlined in
the last two chapters, but his proposed solution is a
definitive separation of 'caring' and 'controlling' functions.
He would like to see the probation service become a
'court-based social work service', providing help on an
essentially voluntary basis for those involved in criminal
or civil court proceedings, leaving to some other service
the development of a range of 'community-based punishments'. These would be explicitly punitive, designed to
offer alternatives to damaging custodial sentences but no
longer hampered by the need to maintain a myth that they
are simultaneously helpful to offenders.

So far, so good, but inevitably we must ask ourselves
how such a 'court-based social work service' could retain
a reasonable level of credibility and funding if it no longer

appeared to be dealing with problems of urgent concern to the criminal justice system. If helping is purely voluntary and on a basis of offenders' needs, what can justify the special treatment of offenders in relation to the needs of other deprived groups in the community? The courts have not proved noticeably willing to allow total discretionary control over the provision of help to offenders to pass into the hands of social workers; this is demonstrated not only by their declining confidence in probation orders from 1972 to 1978, but by the consistent uneasiness of juvenile courts about care orders under the 1969 Children and Young Persons Act which allowed all decisions about the handling of children in care after sentence to be made by local authorities. Recent policy (Home Office 1980) and legislation (the 1982 Criminal Justice Act) have aimed to reverse this trend and to give courts *more* control over the nature of the service provided by social workers to offenders and the conditions under which it is provided. This also reflects a wider public concern that decisions made by social workers which have a substantial effect on clients' lives should be opened up to public scrutiny by a judicial process rather than made in secrecy by 'expert' committees: compare, for instance, the controversy over the powers of local authorities to assume parental rights over children placed in voluntary care (One-Parent Families 1982).

The problem seems to be that by separating the Probation Service's helping function from the criminal justice process Harris may be making it less, rather than more likely that offenders will receive help. It is rather unfair to magistrates and judges to argue as if they are interested only in punishment and never in helping offenders, but the help has to be provided in a way that is relevant to the central concerns of criminal justice if it is to remain an important issue in the decision-making process. Courts, in providing opportunities for help, usually need to do so in ways which are consistent with the community's expectation that they 'do something about' crime and offenders, and sentencers now seem to expect more rather than less control over the conditions of help, particularly when they have to decide under what conditions a person who might otherwise be in custody should be allowed to remain in the community.

On balance, it is tempting to see far better prospects of funding and support for whatever agency will provide Harris' non-custodial 'community punishments'. There have been a number of influential suggestions that the probation service should assume this role and move in a direction precisely opposite to that suggested by Harris. Our next concern is with these attempts to turn the probation service explicitly into a community punishment agency.

ADVISE, ASSIST AND COMPEL?
THE RISE OF 'CONTROLISM'

Few developments in the probation service have attracted so much criticism and hostility from large numbers of its own staff as the attempt to develop 'tougher' and more punitive probation orders in order to increase their attractiveness to courts. Many of the Younger Report's suggestions for tougher probation, such as the Supervision and Control Order giving officers the power to detain offenders in custody for 72 hours if they seemed *likely* to commit a further offence, were resoundingly rejected by the service; however, in the years since Younger we have seen a continuing concern about giving teeth to the probation order, in an attempt to recapture credibility with sentencers who are assumed to want toughness.

A good example of this strategy in practice is the Probation Control Unit opened in 1980 in Kent, where probationers were required to attend six days a week for six months, including evenings, and to conform to curfew regulations when they went home to sleep. If they had jobs, they were to report to the unit straight after work. Before a day off (these were limited to Sundays and Bank

Holidays) the probationer had the conditions of his order read out to him as a reminder. Some extracts from the Unit's rules give the intended flavour of the regime:

There is an expectation that probationers will respond immediately to any lawfully given instruction and the necessity to give any instruction more than twice should be considered as an infringement of the unit's discipline code.

Whilst every effort will be made to encourage good relationships between staff and probationers, there should always be clear lines of demarcation. Probationers will at all times address members of staff using their correct titles and surnames.

It must be clearly understood by staff and explained to probationers that such procedures are not intended to be a mindless response to authority. On the contrary, such procedures will be used quite deliberately in the unit to protect probationers from the danger of becoming overfamiliar with staff. Such familiarity could at some stage endanger a probationer's liberty through misunderstanding. (Kent Probation and After-Care Service 1981)

Breaches of discipline were to be punished by extra community service on Saturdays, or in extreme cases breach proceedings. Documents describing the unit explicitly emphasised containment and deterrence, and there was little reference to any procedures or practices designed to assess clients' needs or provide appropriate help. Only one of the staff was a qualified probation officer, as the majority of staff roles were not seen as requiring social work training.

The introduction of this unit attracted immediate and strongly felt criticism from officers who saw it as incompatible with social work traditions, as well as from directors of the four experimental Day Training Centres set up under the 1972 Criminal Justice Act, who aimed to provide useful help to offenders through a trained staff team and were alarmed at the prospect of units requiring longer attendance under more punitive conditions when their own centres did not seem to be attracting Home Office support. Other commentators welcomed the Kent development as realistic and positive. For instance, Martin Davies, who had been closely involved in the Home Office Research Unit's programme of probation research and wrote a number of its reports, told chief probation officers that the service should provide 'a non-custodial disposal that will be seen not only as an acceptable option to prison, but as a punitive, retributive and controlling facility in its own right, hard enough to replace prison as the preferred short-term sentence. . . . Such a provision should involve day-long containment for five or even seven days a week' (Davies 1982).

The Kent Control Unit has been jokingly described as a non-residential prison, but in reality there was a good deal of thought behind it. Even if it turned out less harsh in practice than the plans suggested, its implications need to be considered seriously. If the probation service could legitimately operate a facility of this kind as part of a probation order, could it also run weekend prisons? What considerations limit the range of controls which can be imposed as conditions of a probation order? Extra conditions in probation orders are nothing new in themselves. In the USA they have been developed into an impressive array of powers, including in many states the option of imposing a period in custody as an integral part of probation. An article by Harry Joe Jaffe, an American probation officer, describes some more unusual conditions, including restrictions on rights of free speech, association and assembly. Various forms of reparation and community service can be included, as can more detailed regulation of everyday life such as to 'belong to no Irish organisation, cultural or otherwise; not to visit any Irish pubs'. Some probationers are required to submit themselves at any time to searches without warrant, and one bag snatcher was required to 'wear leather shoes with metal taps on the heels and toes anytime he leaves the house', instead of the tennis shoes he normally wore to sneak up on his victims (Jaffe 1979). The same spirit is expressed by an American assistant director of corrections, in an article entitled 'Probation: call it control, and mean it' (Barkdull 1976: 'the public image of probation means getting off') and by a British chief probation officer arguing for an explicit philosophy of 'containment' (Griffiths 1982). However, in America there are some limitations. Conditions must 'conform with the constitutional rights of the probationer and the limits of the probation statute' (Jaffe 1979). The Federal Probation Act is seen as having a bilateral nature, involving protection of the public and help to the offender, and some requirements have been deleted by appellate courts on the grounds that they are merely restrictive and have no rehabilitative purpose.

Under British law, in the absence of a constitutional definition of rights, the position was not so clear. When the Kent Control Unit was set up, the powers of probation officers were defined mainly by the Powers of Criminal Courts Act 1973, which contained an unfortunate ambiguity. Section 4 of the Act contained provision for attendance at a day training centre as a condition of probation, but with very clear limitations. Attendance was limited to three months and was available only in areas where designated centres existed (London, Liverpool, Sheffield and Pontypridd). Confusingly, section 2 of the same Act contained a general power to require probationers to 'comply with such requirements as the court . . . considers necessary for securing the good conduct of the offender'. Courts in Kent and elsewhere interpreted section 2 as allowing them to order six months' attendance at the control unit and similar facilities. To others it seemed at least doubtful if this section was intended to permit requirements even more restrictive than those specifically created *and limited* in section 4, or why bother with section 4 at all? In practice, however, the letter of the law appeared to set few boundaries. Did this mean that section 2 could be used to create a wide range of what were virtually new sentences, without public debate or specific legislation? Were the options in any way limited by a probation officer's legal duty to 'advise, assist and befriend' those under his supervision?

For a short while, it did indeed look as if 'controlism' had run into substantial legal obstacles. In 1981 a probationer who had been ordered to attend a day centre in North Shields (*not* a designated centre under the 1973 Act) as a condition of her order was successfully prosecuted for failure to attend, and then appealed against the magistrate's finding on the grounds that the condition was invalid. The divisional court upheld the appeal, and the matter was pursued with Home Office encouragement to the House of Lords, where to many people's surprise the divisional court's ruling was upheld and the condition ruled invalid (Cullen v. Rogers, House of Lords 1982). This confirmed some people's previous doubts about the legality of such conditions (Raynor 1982), but the reasoning of the judgement was particularly interesting in that it attempted to lay down some general principles governing what was appropriate for inclusion in a probation order. Lord Bridge of Harwich took the view that 'a requirement . . . must not introduce such a custodial or other element as will amount in substance to the imposition of a sentence', and that 'the discretion conferred on the probation officer . . . must itself be confined within well-defined limits'. A requirement of the wide-ranging and general kind imposed on Rogers was held invalid 'on the ground both that it would involve a substantial element of custodial punishment and that it would subject the probationer to the unfettered discretionary control of the probation officer'.

This judgement, welcomed by many for its restatement of the principle that probation is 'instead of sentence', caused a considerable stir. Although Lord Bridge clearly had in mind mainly requirements to attend daily at centres not specified as day training centres, many courts and probation committees became worried about the validity of *any* unusual requirement, including requirements to attend various groupwork or activity projects for only a few hours a week. Home Office officials could give little guidance and some projects were shelved, or re-opened on a voluntary basis which gave the courts no guarantee that attendance would be enforced. Projects with 'social work' aims were as vulnerable as purely deterrent or punitive projects. Some courts developed a commendable practice of closely specified and limited requirements, such as 'to attend the X scheme (being a non-custodial group therapy scheme held as and where instructed by the group leader). Such attendance shall not extend beyond 12 months and shall not exceed six hours in any one week'. In one particularly confusing situation, a Crown court judge advised magistrates' courts to use wording of this kind while another judge at the same court decided that Crown court orders relating to the same project could only be made on a basis of voluntary attendance. Meanwhile the project staff held a series of worried meetings with local court officials to try to determine whether they could still bring breach actions in case of non-attendance.

The pragmatic Home Office reaction to this state of affairs, instead of giving guidance based on Lord Bridge's comments about the *purpose* of probation orders, concentrated on legislative tinkering with the Criminal Justice Bill then passing through Parliament on its way to becoming the 1982 Criminal Justice Act. What emerged was a power to make requirements to attend at a particular location or participate in a specified activity for not more than 60 days. Courts have to be satisfied about the feasibility of such requirements before imposing them, and the local probation committee has to approve facilities for use in connection with such requirements.

This kind of formulation will do something to limit long or unspecified periods of daily attendance like the six months' requirement of the Kent Control Unit or the unlimited requirement in Cullen v. Rogers, but it does little to define the purpose of such requirements and provides as many opportunities for controlling and punitive projects as for projects with positive aims. Responsibility for determining these issues is passed to local committees and their staff. But on what basis should they decide whether or not to set up punitive and deterrent projects?

Contributors to the *Probation Journal* and to the left-wing probation officers' publication *Probe* have linked increasing 'controlism' to a number of other developments. Penal policymakers have been actively interested in 'strengthened' (i.e. more coercive) non-custodial sentences since the publication of the Younger Report, and a Conservative political climate may favour 'toughness' in probation as it does in detention centres. Some officers have argued that the social work base of the probation service's activities has been eroded by the runaway success of community service orders, which involve supervision without specific social work aims, and usually by staff who are not qualified in social work. Others have suggested that as probation areas have become larger, management risks becoming more remote and bureaucratic, and may react to scepticism about the value of social work by emphasising the concrete and quantifiable and becoming preoccupied with rules and routines (Burnham 1981). The concept of 'need' itself is ambiguous and does not help to clarify the issue: 'he needs to be controlled' is not necessarily a statement about *his* needs at all. The whole argument risks being seen as a stereotypical conflict between 'hardliners' and 'wets', but research and experience do suggest some good reasons for scepticism.

Measures which are designed as 'alternatives to custody' often fail effectively to divert offenders from prison. Suspended sentences are a familiar example (Bottoms 1980) and recent research has revealed the failure of most

intermediate treatment to divert juvenile offenders from
residential care (Thorpe, Smith, Green and Paley 1980).
Even community service orders seem to operate as
alternatives to prison only about half the time; the other
half are alternatives to fines or probation (Pease and
McWilliams 1980). Toughness and authoritarianism may
not by themselves guarantee that courts will use a
particular facility only or mainly for people who would
otherwise have gone to prison. On the other hand,
unpublished research on the day training centres suggests
that they were used mainly as alternatives to prison, while
remaining relatively flexible and client-centred (Willis
1979). We should not simply assume that toughness is
either a sufficient or a necessary condition of credibility.

There should also be some doubt about the effectiveness of more intensive supervision. Closer surveillance
will not necessarily do any good unless it also involves the
use of effective methods of help. Both British and
American researchers have produced examples of intensi-
fied supervision actually proving counterproductive
(Folkard, Smith and Smith 1976; Adams 1967), and a
multiplication of special requirements unrelated to clients'
assessed needs may simply lead to higher breach rates.
Effective social work depends partly on compatibility
between the help offered and the client's own view of his
problems and goals. This will be difficult to achieve in
programmes which allow little space for clients' points of
view or for the negotiation of agreed objectives.

It is not enough simply to base objection to controlism,
as some have done, on 'the social work traditions of the
service'. Unless it can be shown that social work skills
have some relevance to criminal justice objectives, and
not simply to the preferred practice or preferred
professional self-image of a particular occupational group,
it is difficult to argue that sentencers should pay serious
attention to social workers' points of view in the criminal
justice system. On the other hand, if we follow the
'controlists' and relegate social work to a subsidiary role

or to some dwindling residual subsection of the probation service, we are left with very few guidelines about the limits of movement in the direction of purely negative controls.

It is, however, easy to see how the social control orientation commends itself. If coercion can no longer be justified in terms of its effects on offenders as an aid to therapeutic rehabilitation, at least it may have an effect on sentencers by persuading them to use a new facility. If the goals and objectives of the service are no longer defined in social work terms, this leaves the way open to measure success simply by bureaucratic means, counting the number of people processed through particular facilities without asking why or with what result. But how far can a social work agency depart from its traditional client-centred focus before it becomes just another controlling arm of the State? And why do you need probation officers, with their particular training and interests, to operate such an agency?

Some probation officers have made an explicit attempt to spell out the relationship of the probation service to the State in the context of a Marxist analysis of contemporary capitalist societies. Not surprisingly, they find themselves fundamentally opposed to the 'controlist' solution. It is to their views that we turn next.

SOCIALIST PROBATION

One of the most persistent voices raised against 'controlism' in the probation service has been that of the NAPO Members' Action Group, and any discussion of radical prescriptions for probation practice must start from the recent book by two of its members, *Probation Work: Critical Theory and Socialist Practice* (Walker and Beaumont 1981). This book belongs very clearly in the tradition of the structural critique of social work outlined in the previous chapter, but is untypical in that it contains discussions of everyday practice and suggestions about what socialist probation officers can actually do. (The only other substantial example of this is Bruce Hugman's essay on radical probation work (in Brake and Bailey 1980) which comes to some rather similar conclusions as far as practice is concerned.)

Walker and Beaumont's book also elaborates in detail the theoretical background to their ideas on practice. In the first part they describe a number of areas of contemporary practice, contrasting the confusing every-day reality of the work with official accounts. They draw out the extent to which the official accounts rely on a consensus model of society and on attempts to rehabilitate and reintegrate the offender through a professional casework service. They draw heavily on arguments similar to those reviewed in the last chapter, but the theoretical meat of the book is in its second section, where the authors draw on Marxist theories of the function of the State and its welfare services in capitalist societies and develop an analysis of the probation service along the same lines. Their argument is detailed and sophisticated, and cannot really be summarised here; interested readers are referred to the original. (They will also find there some delightful examples of management responses to radical criticism, such as a chief probation officer who told his staff: 'For some it may be easier to turn from their client's shortcomings and their own imperfections to the imperfections of society . . . This is a stereotype of adolescent thinking, and we all have an adolescent inside us trying to get out.')

Their particular version of Marxism is not the simplistic 'left idealism' of early Case Con, but stresses the complex and contradictory nature of the State in advanced capitalist societies. They argue that the State apparatus seeks legitimacy and consent through the provision of double-edged welfare services which simultaneously provide real benefits for deprived people and also act as a subtle form of social control by encouraging and rewarding compliance with existing social arrangements in a strikingly unequal society. The criminal justice system is analysed as part of the State's apparatus of control, operating through the soft coercion of the probation service backed up by the harder coercion of prisons. In particular, they point to the need from time to time for stronger coercive measures to contain social disorder resulting from the economic malfunctions of the system (as argued for instance by Stuart Hall in his account of the severe response of authorities to 'moral panics' about inner-city crime, in Hall et al. 1978). In this way they link calls for 'tougher probation' with the emergence of tougher policing and the increasing squalor and brutalisation of imprisonment. Their analysis of the probation service's role stresses its double-edged nature: on the one hand, it provides a welfare service which can mitigate and humanise the impact of criminal justice for some offenders; on the other hand, it aims to promote conformity and acceptance of authority, and helps to secure consensual acceptance of oppressive criminal justice by demonstrating that at least part of the system is 'caring'.

Such a brief summary does not do justice to their argument, but its general direction will be clear. Unlike many radical commentators on criminal justice, they recognise that the criminal law is also double-edged: poor people suffer from crime, and their exposure to greater risk through residence in high-crime areas is an important aspect of their socially imposed disadvantage. However, laws to protect property offer more protection to those who have more to protect. Thus the authors do not fall into the trap of romanticising crime as a form of inarticulate social protest, and their focus is on how the probation service can increase its admittedly marginal influence towards progressive social goals while resisting full incorporation into the coercive State machine. In this way they avoid engaging in sterile debates about reformism versus revolution and allow themselves to emerge as frank reformists, albeit still uncomfortable about the extent to which their reforms might help to stabilise the system they oppose. Revealingly, their 'Marxist' critique leads on to a discussion of 'socialist' practice with which non-Marxist socialists could largely agree.

The authors make little attempt to counter possible objections to their Marxist position, remarking simply that 'other explanations are unsatisfactorily superficial and inadequate'. On this level, we take or leave the theory, and non-Marxists will leave it, while Marxists will find it a helpful survival guide through the considerable problems of conscience they encounter when they happen to earn their living as probation officers. The authors' comment that 'socialist probation officers find themselves working within a criminal justice system, much of which they oppose' has a flavour of understatement when set alongside the explicit Marxist analysis which precedes it. But since most probation officers seem to develop their theoretical orientations piecemeal on the basis of eclectic training modified by working experience, the main contribution of a Marxist book to the wider probation debate is probably at the level of its practice ideas. For these purposes, there is no need to make obvious points about the coercive nature of social control in some socialist societies, and it is more constructive to consider the practice suggestions at face value.

These contain a number of hints at a progressive, humane and demystified probation practice. For instance, the authors advocate a realistic attitude to their clients' employment prospects, and a willingness to share with clients a structural approach to the understanding of social problems rather than relying solely on individualised explanations of personal difficulties. Similarly, their awareness of their potential coercive power over clients leads them to emphasise the need to explain the rights and obligations of both parties in the supervisory relationship. They stress that clients should be helped on the basis of the problems which clients themselves define, and that they can be offered useful skills and resources if

officers share knowledge with them and develop 'useful
services'. In most of these recommendations they are
close to some modern developments in mainstream social
work. They also advocate a greater degree of community
involvement with participation in progressive campaigns
in co-operation with pressure groups and sections of the
wider labour movement. Within the service itself, they
advocate the promotion of collective critical debate about
professional issues, combined with a team approach to
practice decisions as a counterbalance to increasing
bureaucracy and hierarchical controls.

Their ideas about practice remain an outline, but
constitute a useful contribution to the debate. In so far as
they depend on Marxist assumptions, they are likely to
remain a minority position, but where they have much in
common with other progressive developments in social
work they can probably attract a wider constituency of
support, as they have already done among active members
of the National Association of Probation Officers.
Although it is still difficult to imagine a strong base for
Marxist social work developing within the criminal justice
system, there is much to be learned from their emphasis
on the relative autonomy of probation officers within the
system and their capacity to affect its operation if they
have a coherent strategy. The target for influence may
not be simply the offender himself but also the system
which processes and sentences him, and although such
change is likely to be gradual and reformist, a structural
understanding is important in opening our eyes to these
possibilities. Walker and Beaumont point out that 'it
matters that there are *probation officers* prepared to state
publicly that prison is destructive, that there are unjust
laws, that law enforcement is discriminatory and even
that the probation service cannot cope with the poverty
and hardship our work uncovers'. It matters even more
that they should be prepared to take advantage of
whatever opportunities arise to influence this state of
affairs, however marginally.

'SENTENCED TO SOCIAL WORK':
COMPULSORY SUPERVISION WITH
VOLUNTARY HELP

Questions about the potential influence of the probation service on the everyday operations of the criminal justice system need to be tackled not only at the level of theory and of probation officers' work with their clients, but also at the level of their influence on actual sentencing decisions. If courts make many of their routine sentencing decisions on the basis of an informal tariff of perceived seriousness and graduated severity of response, where does the probation order fit into the tariff? Should it be a therapeutic measure outside the tariff, with all the attendant risks of increasing marginality and limited impact, or should it be integrated into the tariff system as a realistic alternative sentence? As we have seen, this second strategy leads to fears about 'community punishments' replacing a tradition of helping offenders, but unless the probation order can be seen as having a wide range of application, particularly to offenders who would otherwise risk custodial sentences, its potential contribution to criminal justice will be limited.

One recent and influential attempt at a new framework for probation orders which directly addressed this issue was the paper 'Sentenced to social work' (Bryant et al. 1978), which originally appeared in the *Probation Journal* and re-appeared later as a discussion paper of a regional subcommittee of the Conference of Chief Probation Officers, inspiring some experimental schemes on the way. In essence, the argument put forward by Bryant and his co-authors starts from the same point as Harris's, namely that the traditional pattern of probation orders, with its combination of enforced reporting and an imposed expectation of a social work relationship, tries to do too many things at the same time with resulting confusion about the purposes of the component parts. Instead, however, of arguing for a wholesale separation of caring and controlling functions they argue for a clearer delineation of these aspects within the probation order. They advocate a new form of order in which courts will specify the required degree of surveillance and control by determining the frequency of reporting, while officers and clients establish, by voluntary agreement within this framework, the extent to which they offer and receive a social work service. They see the probation order as involving two 'contracts' or areas of agreement, one (the primary contract) between the probationer and the court which determines the extent to which his freedom will be limited by reporting to probation officers as a consequence of his offence, the other (a subsidiary contract) between the probationer and the service, concerned with assessment of problems and the provision of help. This subsidiary contract would be essentially voluntary, and offenders would no longer risk breach proceedings for 'failing to respond to casework' provided that they observed the basic behavioural requirements of the legal order. Probation officers would be able to offer a range of help without offenders feeling obliged to pretend to accept it unless they genuinely wished to, and officers would be freed to provide better help for those who could use it without being obliged to 'go through the motions' with unwilling clients.

So far, the argument is attractive, suggesting greater honesty and openness between officers and clients about social work decisions while at the same time recognising the reality of the 'reporting order', in which little help is requested or offered — the offender complies with what is seen basically as an inconvenience required by the court. This inconvenience should be seen for what it is, namely a form of punishment rather than a vehicle to ensure therapeutic contact, and should therefore be available within the tariff system as an alternative to more harmful punishments. Bryant et al. would prefer the court to determine the appropriate level of punishment and other more appropriate channels to make the social work choices, allowing some offenders to accept probation purely as punishment without being 'sentenced to social work'.

The difficulties begin to emerge at the level of translation into practice. Critics who objected to the rather routine and sterile nature of the probation order envisaged for the non-social-work cases perhaps underestimated the degree of sterility and routinisation suggested by consumer studies of traditional probation orders (Davies 1979), but some of the administrative arrangements suggested by Bryant et al. seemed to move a long way towards the conscious institutionalisation of a routine approach. For instance, they suggested that the probationer, after one interview with a probation officer to explain and discuss the social work services available, report thereafter to a 'receptionist' who would duly record that he had reported, and that this would be the nature of his continuing contact with the agency unless he specifically asked to see a probation officer. Breach action could be virtually automatic following a specified number of failures to report, and officers' traditional discretion in this area would be reduced. (Waiting rooms, however, were to be made more 'bright and colourful', with posters describing the various forms of help available in case probationers wished to follow them up). In practice, experiments with this type of probation order have considerably modified these guidelines, and some of the reported experiences with this model will be discussed later.

The authors of this paper were understandably concerned with ways of selling the probation order to courts as a credible sentence which need not be restricted to the obvious traditional 'social work cases' and rightly pointed to the fact that the service is increasingly involved in implementing measures where the social work purpose is not primary, such as community service orders. Two major questions however, need further consideration. First, what is the content of a 'reporting only' order? What is left of a probation order if you extract the 'social work' bit, and is what remains enough to constitute a 'credible sentence'? Community service is not an exact parallel, since a community service order has its own distinctive and constructive content of a prescribed amount of unpaid work for the general benefit of the community. Secondly, does the model really offer significant opportunities for clients to make informed choices about making use of available help when they are likely to be unfamiliar with the possible forms of help, and will not necessarily have arrived unaided at a clear picture of their own difficulties and of what might be done about them? On the face of it, there is a danger that making clients responsible for requesting help might lessen the motivation of officers to extend their range of skills and resources to cope with a wider range of need, if the probationer is invited to respond only to what is already offered. Courts often seem to make probation orders partly to ensure that a 'strong' offer of help is made to a defendant who has in the past shown little interest in 'weak' offers. Whether or not this is a realistic aspiration for sentencers (and certainly they would be unrealistic to see probation as a *guarantee* of help), to weaken the link between probation orders and help may paradoxically lessen their attraction for courts in these cases. Answers to this kind of question require a much more detailed consideration of the process of negotiation between the officer and the probationer as potential social work client, and careful thought about how people come to engage themselves in recognising problems and accepting help.

PROBATION WITHOUT 'TREATMENT'

We turn now to the most systematic recent attempt to outline a possible role within the criminal justice system for a probation service which can no longer claim to offer effective 'treatments for delinquency'. This is to be found in the proposed 'non-treatment paradigm' (Bottoms and McWilliams 1979), which suggested that the probation service cease to rely on 'treatment' claims and concentrate instead on four traditional aims:

1 the provision of appropriate help to offenders;
2 the statutory supervision of offenders;
3 diverting appropriate offenders from custodial sentences;
4 the reduction of crime.

The authors' detailed argument is mainly concerned with the first three aims; the fourth is less developed, resting on some suggestive examples of community development linked to crime prevention, and they acknowledge a need for more thorough consideration of this issue. However, our main concern at this point is with the development of their concept of 'help' and its application within criminal justice. Briefly, they suggest that in both probation and after-care work the service should cease to interpret its activities as 'treatment for crime' and instead should aim to provide help in relation to client-defined problems. They neatly encapsulate the necessary logical and philosophical shifts in schematic form:

(a) Treatment   becomes   help.
(b) Diagnosis   becomes   shared assessment.
(c) Client's dependent   becomes   Collaboratively
     need as the basis   defined task as the
     for social work   basis for social
     action   work action.

Thus by abandoning the 'medical model' of social work help, with its implications of expert one-sided diagnosis and of treatment as something done by experts *to* passive and objectified clients, they suggest that many of the dangers of negative labelling, and of failing to draw on clients' own potential for informed choice and constructive change, can be avoided. Similarly this model could provide some safeguards against the injustice which can arise when clients are in effect punished for failure to respond to a 'treatment' which was based on the officer's unilateral decision rather than on any agreement with the client. Also within the supervisory process itself they hope to avoid 'encouraging the differential enforcement of the requirements of probation orders according to rather unreliable judgements of response to treatment'. In this their thinking is very close to that of Bryant et al. (1978).

Applying these principles to the role of the service in criminal justice, their 'four aims' can be justified as follows. The goal of providing help to offenders can be legitimated by general principles relating to the value of persons and the fact that many offenders are disadvantaged people experiencing considerable difficulties both within and outside the criminal justice system. The general principle of providing help to people in need is embodied in the consensus ideology of the Welfare State, and would initially seem to need no special separate justification in the context of criminal justice. The statutory supervision of offenders is a traditional expectation of the courts, which gives probation officers an inescapable law enforcement role and determines the limiting conditions within which their offers of help can be made. The authors argue for a supervisory practice which maximises client choice within these limits. The third aim of providing and developing diversionary resources is justified by the excessive use of pointless and destructive custodial sentences, much of it incidentally rationalised in 'treatment' terms ('Your worships may well consider that this young man would benefit from a structured environment' is a treatment-language way of saying 'Send him to Borstal'). The fourth aim, reducing crime, is one which commands wide agreement anyway although we know little about how to achieve it. It is better to recognise this ignorance than to pretend that we routinely provide 'treatments'.

The main argument is persuasively stated, and I would

agree with most of it. However, there are some gaps and difficulties which must limit its usefulness as a guide to action for social workers and probation officers. In general, it tells us more clearly what to avoid than what to do instead, and many details of the argument have been criticised. It is not clear that in practice probation officers or social workers operate exclusively within a 'treatment' paradigm, and the development of social work over the last ten years has provided plenty of good reasons for not doing so. For instance, Hardiker's research (1977) on the practice ideologies embodied in social inquiry reports showed that officers vary between 'treatment' and 'non-treatment' principles in their recommendations. Hardiker's categories seem to reflect the distinction between 'individualised' sentencing based on the offender's characteristics and 'tariff' sentencing based on classical retributive principles and do not, therefore, correspond precisely to Bottoms and McWilliams's differentiation between 'treatment' and 'non-treatment', since their 'non-treatment' category clearly includes individualised 'helping' provided that the help is not based on a medical model; however, as Harris (1980) points out, Hardiker's evidence supports other observations that probation officers are not consistently dominated by a 'treatment' paradigm, and officers certainly do a lot of 'helping' (Willis 1983). But Bottoms and McWilliams's main point is not that probation officers routinely practise 'treatment' so much as that their work is routinely presented and understood as 'treatment', and that the role of the probation service in criminal justice has been legitimated and rationalised on 'treatment' grounds. Many social inquiry reports and officers' records reflect the resulting tendency to recast ordinary experience into social-work-diagnostic 'treatment' language, as if 'helping' were somehow an unofficial activity which has to be represented as 'treatment' to make it respectable. A man may need a home because he is homeless, or because it is part of a programme of 'treatment' for his delinquency; the problem arises when we feel obliged to confuse the two, and his reoffending in his new home is regarded as a failure of 'treatment' requiring new and more drastic 'treatment' measures. The initial argument, that probation officers' decisions and practices should no longer be justified by reference to a 'treatment model' and in fact do not require such justification, is strengthened rather than weakened by the observation that *in practice* much of probation work does not fit the 'treatment' description.

Other criticisms have focused on the 'community' dimension and argued that 'community involvement' can become 'community surveillance', echoing the concern of radical sociologists that official control of daily life can be subtly extended from institutions into the community by 'diversion' programmes without changing its essential nature (Cohen 1979). Of course this is a danger to be recognised in the design and implementation of any community development work directed towards crime prevention or social integration — integration on whose terms? But this again does not seem to affect the central argument, and it is in any case likely that the subtle extension of control is more insidious and less easily seen if it is disguised by the rhetoric of 'treatment'. A more difficult problem arises in the area of the third aim: diversion of offenders from custody. Can any 'alternative to custody', involving whatever degree of control short of actual imprisonment, be justified as 'more helpful' simply on the grounds that it replaces a more restrictive custodial sentence? Do control units become unequivocally helpful, and a legitimate activity for the probation service, as soon as it is demonstrated that they actually divert? Although no such demonstration has yet been achieved, it is certainly possible in principle. Is this sufficient to fit such facilities within the broad category of 'help', or does the concept of 'help' require a more direct reflection of clients' perceptions of their own difficulties and interests? If 'helpfulness' in the context of diversion can be defined simply as diversionary efficacy this is rather different from the client-centred focus of the rest of the argument, and gives little guidance as to the appropriate content of diversionary programmes. Does it matter if clients dig ditches all day so long as they are not in prison?

The only solution suggested by Bottoms and McWilliams to this problem is that since credible alternatives to custody must often involve an element of explicit control which is not likely to reflect client's own perceptions of their needs, programmes involving substantial controls should only be suggested in social inquiry reports if the suggestion is made with the client's consent — a principle which they would extend to all 'recommendations' in reports. This goes some way to resolving the difficulty, and they stress that such consent must not become a routine formality amounting to the rubber-stamping of a coercive process, but we are left with problems rather similar to those raised by the 'sentenced to social work' model. What *in practice* is involved in ensuring that choices made in difficult situations with incomplete information are 'genuine' choices? What role does the non-treatment paradigm envisage for social work principles and social workers' skills in the process of negotiation between officer and potential client? Clearly these skills are not to be used simply to persuade, but to allow a well-informed and realistic exercise of choice based on a clear appreciation of circumstances and their constraints and possibilities, including the demands of criminal justice for an element of control. These problems of practice receive little detailed consideration in the 'non-treatment' approach which then runs the risk of being dismissed by practitioners as little more than an academic or semantic argument. In any case, why should the criminal justice system be so interested in offering choices to offenders?

A significant attempt to draw some of these contending models together into guidelines for policy and practice has been made in a report (NAPO 1981) which, with its stress on campaigning for positive reforms in criminal justice, a reduction in custodial sentencing and a practice informed by a social work focus on the problems and needs of offenders, should attract a large measure of agreement among probation officers. However, this chapter has illustrated some central problems emerging from the theoretical debate which can be summed up as problems about the role and function of social work practice within the criminal justice system. The NAPO document attempts some definition in this area:

> The uniqueness of the Probation Service is that it offers social work help to offenders while giving particular attention to their offending as well as other factors. This social work identity and our role in providing help to people who have committed or are accused of crimes and who are involved in the legal and penal system is basic. Our practice enables us to develop expertise and skill in discerning and dealing with the implications of an individual's criminality. In particular we develop an appreciation of the procedures and practices of the police, the courts and the prisons.

Such a statement identifies neatly the probation service's particular location and opportunities, but it is less clear how these are related to issues like the extent to which coercive controls can be exercised under a probation order, or the extent to which social workers in criminal justice are part of a system of punishment. The report argues that 'the use of methods of containment or surveillance as part of the supervision of the Order are [*sic*] quite inappropriate', and elsewhere that 'for the Probation Service to seek to impose such control on individual offenders would involve an unacceptable change in the principles and ethos of our work'. These views attract a good deal of support, and the document is to be commended as a clear statement of a 'helping' approach to probation and by implication to other aspects of social work in criminal justice. But in the last analysis they are based simply on the preferences of probation officers to work in particular ways, as if criminal justice is being invited to expect a social work approach because probation officers prefer it that way, rather than as an essential part of what the criminal justice system itself needs in order to perform its own essential tasks better.

What does criminal justice need from social work? The survival of social work, including the activities of the probation service, as a necessary part of the administration of justice depends on some demonstration that it helps the criminal justice system itself to perform its functions for the community. It is not sufficient to show that it meets certain needs of offenders or social workers. The essential question is, how can social work be provided within the criminal justice system in a way which is not only helpful to offenders, but ensures its own continued legitimation and support by improving the quality of criminal justice from the point of view of other significant parties as well as offenders? 'Controlism' seeks to substitute system goals for offenders' needs, and radicalism does the reverse; the problem is to articulate a practice which goes some way to meeting both kinds of need.

'Non-treatment', with its emphasis on negotiation, responsibility and informed choice, is a step in this direction but leaves out the details of what might constitute a social work practice to achieve these aims. Filling these gaps requires some consideration not only of the relevance of social work procedures and values to the goals of criminal justice but also a recognition of some of the current problems of the criminal justice system itself. If the probation service is left confused about its goals by the demise of 'rehabilitation through casework', the criminal justice system is in similar disarray through the failure of a sentencing policy based on correctional and rehabilitative assumptions. If social work and criminal justice are to remain in significant contact both require some reappraisal of functions and aims. The next part of this discussion explores some traditional and modern concerns in social work practice and relates these to some contemporary dilemmas in criminal justice.

PART II

Social Work Goals in Criminal Justice

I have ever been of opinion that the greater part of mankind do approximately know where they get that which does them good.

Samuel Butler, 'Erewhon', chapter XV

4

Social Work and Clients' Choices

When social workers and probation officers complain, as we have seen that they do, that their involvement in coercive criminal justice conflicts with their 'social work identity', what do they mean? Clearly they are trying to do more than simply to state a preference for particular ways of working or for a particular professional self-image. They are appealing to values or ethical presuppositions which they regard as central to their work, without which the work becomes something entirely different. These values are notoriously difficult to state clearly, and are often confused; in particular, much of the first part of this book points to a continuing confusion between kinds of activity which can conveniently be labelled 'help' and 'treatment'. It has been suggested that the concept of treatment invokes false analogies between social work and medicine; between crime and disease; and between social or moral problems and physiological malfunctions (Flew 1973). Some of the writers whose work is reviewed in the last chapter argue that a commitment to treatment has encouraged social workers in the criminal justice field to neglect the common-sense perceptions of offenders and sentencers who regard offending as a matter of voluntary choice, and to neglect the importance of clients' own decisions and wishes in the treatment process. Treatment provides a rationalisation for social workers' involvement in coercion, but its effectiveness is questionable. It has been correctly pointed out that social workers and probation officers were providing help long before they came to see themselves (or were encouraged to see themselves) as psychosocial therapists providing treatment. But for many the distinction between help and treatment remains blurred; 'treatment' itself is used carelessly both as a general term for any course of action adopted towards a person ('that's no way to treat a lady') and as a more specific term denoting actions chosen on the basis of expert knowledge to remedy some diagnosed ill ('treat your walls for damp'; 'psychopathy is not treatable'). In so far as social work has claimed to offer professional 'treatment' for social ills, it is the more specific use of the term which is in question, and which Bottoms and McWilliams contrast with 'help'. A simple example, far removed from social work, may help to illustrate the distinctions.

HELPING AND TREATMENT: BOY SCOUTS AND OLD LADIES

Imagine a boy scout returning home in frustration, his good deed for the day not yet performed through lack of suitable opportunities. He sees an elderly lady apparently hesitating by a busy road. Filled with enthusiasm, he holds up the traffic and bundles her across to the other side. Has he helped her? A simple answer is: not unless she actually wanted to cross. If he misinterpreted her hesitation (she was simply thinking about something) then he has not helped her but assaulted and coerced her. An objective measure of outcome (whether she arrives at the other side) does not help us to determine whether she has been helped unless we know something of her own wishes and goals. Nor can the boy scout claim his action as 'effective treatment for inability to cross roads', however efficiently and economically he got her across, unless we also have good reason to believe that she *wanted* to cross the road but could not.

Suppose, however, that the lady is lost. She knows

where she wants to go, but is not sure if she needs to cross this road to get there. Suppose the boy scout knows where she is going (he recognises her and knows that she is on her way to a regular appointment with the doctor, but has recently been rehoused and does not yet know her way around). If he acts as originally described, has he helped her? If he knows, expertly, that she needs to cross, but she does not know this, her reaction on reaching the other side may be to resent his unrequested interference, which she will interpret as an assault. If she is a lady of spirit, she may well cross back again under her own steam before deciding what to do next. The boy's action will not be perceived as help, nor be effective as help, unless he has first explained why he is doing it and secured her agreement. (It might, of course, be legitimated retrospectively if she recognises her surroundings after being dragged across, but even then it would perhaps have been better to explain first.) The perceived helpfulness of the action here depends not simply on helper and client having similar objectives but on their knowledge that they are similar, and a 'treatment' model relying on the one-sided expert diagnosis may neglect to involve the client in this way.

In a more complicated case, suppose that she knows what she wants to do (she wants to collect her pension) but, because of her recent rehousing, is not sure where to find the post office, and does not know whether she needs to cross the road to find it. Now she will be even more dependent on the boy scout's expertise and he is in a good position to offer effective expert help, but once again his action will be perceived as unhelpful, and may turn out in practice unhelpful, unless he explains what he is doing and establishes that it coincides with her own goals. To do this he will need to find out first what she is trying to do and why it is difficult.

So far, the example is straightforward enough. It makes no sense to claim that a person has been helped to do something unless that 'something' is relevant to achieving the person's own goals. If this relevance is absent, she has not been 'helped' but made to do it. A 'treatment' model can blur this distinction or at least fail to direct our attention to it. Unless the boy scout's actions respect his client's own view of the world and her capacity to form her own intentions and make her own choices he risks being very unhelpful. He has in this way begun to touch on serious issues which traditionally figure large in the social work literature — client self-determination, and respect for persons.

RESPECT FOR PERSONS AND RESPECT FOR CHOICES

The concept of 'respect for persons' has been thoroughly explored recently by moral philosophers with particular reference to its application in social work and social welfare (Plant 1970; Downie and Telfer 1969 and 1980). Plant points out that 'it is one thing to emphasise the place of this value in casework theory, quite another to give it any precise content'. However, several themes can be identified in (or disentangled from) recent writing on this subject. These themes, or strands of argument, can be summarised as respect for persons as rational beings; respect for persons as moral agents; and respect for persons as ends in themselves, having inherent value rather than simply instrumental usefulness as means to other ends. These themes are interconnected and logically linked to each other, but for clarity they can initially be considered separately.

The idea that we need to have a form of respect for the rationality of other persons if we are to have any organised social life at all rests on the observation that communication with others is a crucial constituent of our social experience. Rational communication requires that we make certain assumptions about the rationality of others, in that it presupposes a basis of shared meanings and shared logical rules at least to a sufficient degree to allow some mutual understanding. We have to expect that other people are, in certain important respects, similar to ourselves if our communications are to be meaningful rather than mere noise. Of course meanings may not be (usually are not?) precisely shared, and misunderstanding is frequent, but the possibility of communication depends on the possibility of understanding. (Even the deliberate creation of misunderstanding through lying presupposes a general pattern of attempted truthful communication, since lying cannot be effective unless people mistake it for truth.) Our everyday assumption that other people have consciousness and a degree of rationality and that we inhabit a world of shared meanings appears to be a necessary condition for much of our social behaviour, and particularly our use of language.

However, it is one thing to argue that the facts of social experience involve a certain kind of respect for or recognition of the shared humanity of other persons, and quite another to argue that we therefore ought to treat them with a particular kind of concern or consideration. The first argument rests on statements about how things are, and factual statements can be true or false; they are in principle testable from our observations of the world. The second argument is normative, concerned with how things ought to be, and normative statements are not statements of fact: they may enjoin or exhort or express preferences, but they do not describe. Ever since Hume's denunciation of attempts to argue from 'is' to 'ought' (Hume 1740) philosophers have been properly wary of attempting to derive normative from factual statements, and the notion of respect for others as moral agents requires some further justification than the simple fact of shared social experience. (It is also observable that people often interact with others whom they do not therefore regard as entitled to the same consideration as themselves. Slave societies or racist societies, where social behaviour is organised around an ideology which denies fully human status to some members, provide obvious examples of this and other examples are not hard to find, for instance in the treatment of women by men.)

This does not mean that there are no relevant connections between the 'facts' of social experience and questions of social values. Plant, for instance, has suggested that when we analyse a social system into the roles played by its participants, the notion of 'role' often implies not simply a pattern of behaviour but a set of obligations which belong to the role and are part of its meaning (consider such role concepts as 'parent' or 'teacher'). If there are shared conventions and expectations about role-performance we can 'read off' and state the moral obligations attached to a particular role (Plant 1970). Can 'social worker' be considered as a role in this way? Some writers, particularly Howe (1980), have argued that social work is in fact best understood as a role-job, that is, a job defined by the distinctive functions of social workers in service delivery rather than by any distinctive and unique set of skills. Taken together with Plant's comments on roles, this suggests that if a distinctive part of a social worker's characteristic function is to secure the co-operation of their clients rather than to compel them, this requires them to recognise and take into account their clients' capacity for self-direction and choice — a form of respect for persons as moral agents, capable of making their own judgements about the rights and wrongs of a course of action. Procedures which seek to create an element of voluntary co-operation necessarily involve a respect for people's capacity to co-operate voluntarily. A social worker's role often requires him to proceed in this way, partly on the very practical grounds that voluntary co-operation is more likely to produce lasting change than coercive measures which may cease to be effective against unwilling victims as soon as the compulsion ceases.

More generally, it has also been argued that respect for persons is a fundamental or necessary condition of any kind of social morality which can be properly regarded as a subject of moral discussion or argument. Downie and Telfer (1969), for instance, suggest that 'respect for persons is the ultimate principle presupposed in our ordinary judgments of social morality', and Plant (1970) that 'respect for persons is not just a moral principle; on the contrary, it is a presupposition of having a moral principle at all'. Plant supports his position by arguing that what is distinctive about moral principles (as opposed, for instance, to custom or habit) is that they can be supported by rational moral argument, and that the possibility of rational assent to moral arguments requires that moral arguments be governed by the normal rules of rationality. For instance, he points out that if we agree with a person because of his skin colour or his social class this cannot be regarded as a rational agreement since it ignores the 'principle of impartiality'. Rational acceptance of an argument is based on the validity of the argument, not on some contingent property of the person who advances it. Rational moral discussion involves a form of respect for the capacity of others to advance rational moral arguments. Thus, for Plant 'morality involves the notion of rational assent; this presupposes impartiality, which in turn involves the concept of respect for persons.' In this way we begin to see a necessary connection between respect for persons as rational beings and respect for persons as moral agents, capable of having reasons for their own actions and of making judgements about their rightness or wrongness.

If respect for persons as actual or potential moral agents is a necessary presupposition of our ordinary ways of discussing moral issues and arriving at decisions about what ought to be done, it can also be shown that respect for persons is necessarily connected with the notion of choice. Statements about the morality of an action normally apply to our voluntary actions only. It makes little sense to debate the rightness or wrongness of an involuntary sneeze, or to ask whether a person acted rightly or wrongly in being forcibly kidnapped. Strawson

(1968) has shown how deterministic assumptions which deny responsibility for voluntary actions would be incompatible with our ordinary social experience by making nonsense of such familiar notions as resentment, blame, or breaking a promise, since all these presuppose a degree of voluntary control over some of our behaviour and make no sense if applied to involuntary behaviour. These features of ordinary moral language are contrasted with what he calls the 'objective attitude' which regards persons as objects or things, reducing their behaviour to symptoms. Some of these problems have been mentioned in the earlier discussion of diagnostic and medical models of social work which tend to reify people and invalidate their own reasons for action: 'patient engages in writing behaviour' is a good example of Strawson's 'objective attitude'. But these arguments also have a particular application to social workers involved in the field of criminal justice.

This has been most clearly spelt out by Flew (1973) who draws a clear distinction, for which he claims a sound basis in everyday experience, between involuntary 'motions' (like the knee-jerk reflex) and voluntary 'movings' (like a deliberate kick). Crime, he argues, belongs characteristically to the voluntary category, unlike involuntary behaviour resulting from mental illness or incapacity. Thus it makes sense to connect crime with notions of responsibility or blame, and mental illness with notions of treatment, but not the other way around. (He also, incidentally, warns us away from a tempting red herring by reminding us that when we describe an action as voluntary, we are not thereby invoking some grand metaphysical speculation about whether it may be possible to give meaningful causal accounts of the action's antecedents, but are simply distinguishing it from involuntary behaviour or behaviour under compulsion.) One implication of Flew's arguments is that probation officers and other social workers in criminal justice should be particularly aware of the necessary connection between respect for persons and respect for the capacity to choose — an example of respect for persons as moral agents.

A third major theme in discussions of respect for persons has been the argument that if we respect the inherent value of persons, this implies that we should value them as ends in themselves and as having worth in themselves, rather than valuing them only according to contingent or accidental characteristics such as colour or gender or social class. As Plant puts it, 'what is in question is not some respect owed to a person because of certain obligations attached to the conventional role structure of a particular society (that is, *as* a farmer, priest etc.), but respect for a person *as* a human being' (Plant 1970). Democratic ideologies institutionalise this value in some ways, for instance by allowing each adult one equal vote regardless of contingent characteristics (if we overlook the exclusion, in Britain, of certain groups such as prisoners). But this also points to a contradiction: in many contexts, we also value people differently according to their *usefulness* in serving some further purpose, and this involves valuing them as means, or instruments, rather than as ends in themselves. One such context is provided by capitalist economies, in which people sell their labour power to become instruments in the achievement of other people's purposes.

It has been argued, most forcibly by Halmos, that political activity of all kinds is also characterised by the instrumental approach to persons, since they are mobilised and led towards ends selected for them by political change-agents. He points to a fundamental incompatibility between respect for persons as ends in themselves (which he identifies as the 'personalist' value base of activities such as psychotherapy and social work) and political activities, among which he includes community work. 'Political action . . . cannot embody the styles and sentiments . . . of individualized rapport . . . Political action must divest itself of the particular and individual and must aim at universals as well as collectivities: the political actor handles generic rules, the personalist actor handles unique relationships with persons' (Halmos 1978). Without denying the value or legitimacy of either kind of activity, he argues against attempts to politicise the personal. He sees such attempts as likely to divert practitioners away from a focus on the interests and welfare of their clients and towards a manipulative stance in which clients' interests and wishes take second place to some long-term aim to achieve change in social systems.

This is not the place to list the objections which could be made to the details of Halmos's argument, though it should be noted in passing that both social workers and community workers often need to be simultaneously concerned with clients' interests and with changes in the operation of systems which affect those interests. What is interesting for our present purposes is that Halmos's exposition of a personalist orientation which is incompatible with the manipulative or coercive use of people as instruments closely resembles the misgivings of probation officers and social workers about innovations such as the explicitly punitive and controlling facilities mentioned in the previous chapter. When these are said to conflict with a traditional 'social work identity' because they concentrate on producing certain kinds of effects on systems (e.g. encouraging sentencers to use them) rather than on providing a client-centred service, this clearly points to a preference for personalist rather than instrumental goals.

To sum up, then, this brief discussion of arguments about 'respect for persons': if appeals to a traditional 'social work identity' are to be understood as restatements of the value of respect for persons, this suggests that social work activities which are consistent with this value should respect clients' choices and seek to promote self-direction, rather than adopting a directive or coercive stance in the instrumental pursuit of some further goal. These arguments can be presented not simply as a matter of personal preference but as a logical consequence of a primary concern for persons. In an earlier article, I suggested that

> the only situations in which we can fully control human behaviour are situations in which we exercise coercion, by removing another person's freedom of action through such means as superior physical force, hypnosis or incapacitating drugs. In doing this we also dehumanize him, by removing some essential components of our ordinary idea of a person as an interpreter of reality, a maker of choices and an initiator of actions. . . . Coercion is, in an important sense, an assault on identity, and any repressive, manipulative or exploitative social relations contain elements of such an assault. (Raynor 1978)

Such arguments suggest that a central concern of social work should be to increase people's sense of identity and responsibility by increasing the range of situations in which they have a real choice of how to behave and how to realise their goals — in other words, a social work which respects persons is centrally concerned with liberation rather than with its opposites.

In practice, of course, the dividing line between pesonalist and instrumental concern is not so easy to draw, since neither social workers nor their clients exist in a social vacuum but in a complex network of involvement with other persons in which their choices have consequences for others. This is particularly clear in criminal justice where some clients' free choices have resulted and will result in harm to others, and social workers and probation officers have not seen it as their job to help clients to commit offences. Any attempt to argue consistently from a 'personalist' position in social work has to recognise and confront issues which arise from respect for persons other than the immediate client, and to find some appropriate balance among these competing interests. The arguments associated with the 'treatment model', namely that the interests of clients and society are in the long run identical, have now been widely rejected; they are seen as an expedient rationalisation which only appears plausible if clients' interests are diagnostically restated and transformed by experts into something the client might not recognise. But social workers in the criminal justice system still need some way of coming to terms with conflicts between clients' wishes and other people's interests.

Halmos encounters a similar problem of balance in relation to his 'personal-political dichotomy' in a world which requires both kinds of understanding and both kinds of action. His solution lies in the concept of 'equilibration', a constant attempt to maintain an awareness of contradictory and incompatible positions without seeking to reduce uncertainty by a false and premature 'hybridisation' or fusion: 'hybridisation conceals the ingredients and permanently obfuscates our sociological palate with either a totally politicised or a totally personalised diet.' He advocates 'the cultivation of a measured and composed uncertainty as a creative principle and as a guide to moral decision'. Equilibration is certainly a suggestive concept, but is elaborated by Halmos largely as an attitude and a discipline which should inform the approach of the academic investigator of social affairs — an aid to detachment and to the productive questioning of experience. Social workers and probation officers, faced with the hourly need to make and implement balanced decisions, need a more practical variety of equilibration. In balancing a respect for clients' choices against a need to influence and sometimes to override those choices they particularly need to have clear ideas about when a person is not the best judge of his own interests or welfare, and about when those interests, however accurately judged, must be overridden in the interests of others.

WELFARE AND RATIONAL PREFERENCE

A concern for persons necessarily implies a concern for

their welfare, and immediately we are involved in another set of conceptual difficulties. 'Welfare', like 'need', might refer to a person's own judgement of what will be good for him, or might refer to somebody else's judgement (perhaps an expert's judgement) of what will be in his 'real' interests, what he 'really needs', which may be different from what he thinks he needs, and may indeed be energetically resisted. So much has been written and argued about these problems that it is both impractical and superfluous to do more here than to outline a few of the issues which seem to be particularly relevant to what social workers do. These concern, mainly, differences between situations where 'respecting persons' involves compliance with people's own view of their welfare, and situations where it might not.

A few preliminary observations are needed, and are based partly on the arguments of G. H. Von Wright (1963). My idea of what is good for me seems necessarily connected with my ideas of what will contribute to my happiness. This is not necessarily the same as 'what I want', since I may be able to resist, or decide not to comply with, my immediate wants because they conflict with some aim I see as more important. Similarly 'happiness' does not seem to equate directly with 'pleasure'. As far as my own perception is concerned, my idea of my own good is the same as my idea of my welfare (and, to extend the argument a little, is closely connected with my beliefs about my needs and interests). But we also talk of 'welfare experts', people who know what is good for other people, which implies that I might be mistaken about my welfare or about my own good. If, however, we accept that my choices of what seems good to me are value choices, which express a preference rather than making the kind of statement about the world which can be demonstrably true or false, how can I be mistaken? Are not 'welfare experts' putting themselves in the classically difficult position of arguing from 'is' to 'ought', or from facts to values, in seeking to determine, through their knowledge of facts, what is valuable for another person?

Part of the answer to this problem is that my choices about what will contribute to my welfare do depend partly on facts, in that if I am mistaken or misinformed about the likely effects of my choices I may bring about a state of affairs which is not what I intended and does not contribute to my welfare. Somebody who understood the facts of my situation better could advise me that my proposed action was unlikely to be good for me, on the basis of factual knowledge about what was likely to happen, and perhaps about other opportunities of which I was ignorant. But if my adviser and I have the same knowledge and agree about the facts but still disagree about whether it is desirable that I should act in the way I propose, the difference between us is no longer my deficiency in factual expertise but only our different value preferences. In relation to this difference, he might try to persuade me by moral arguments about the undesirability of my choice, but would no longer be relying on his factual expertise to do so. He would have to admit that I had the factual parts of my decision right, and our disagreement would be about goals and values. If he says I am still wrong, he now means morally wrong not factually wrong, and is indicating that in the same circumstances he, for moral reasons, would have a different preference. As long as the difference between us is about facts, he can be said to be helping me if he persuades me to a different course of action which will actually be more effective in promoting my welfare as I see it. When the difference between us is reduced to one of different moral preferences, his continuing disagreement is no longer so clearly definable as 'help'. He might be trying to convert me, or 'save me from myself', but this could be seen as 'help' only if I came to share his own normative frame of reference.

Brandt (1976) has argued that much of the vagueness and confusion in the way we use the term 'welfare' can be overcome if we consistently bear in mind a central part of its meaning, which he describes as 'rational preference' — in other words, what is good for me, or promotes my welfare, is the same as 'what I rationally prefer'. The concept 'rationally' here needs some unpacking, but among the criteria which would allow us to call a preference rational would be thorough knowledge of the facts of the situation and their causal influences on each other — that is, not being mistaken about facts. Thus our reasons for regarding a preference as irrational and unlikely to contribute to someone's welfare would be based on considerations about how the decision was arrived at rather than about the extent of our agreement with the end result. The kinds of consideration which would indicate an irrational preference seem to be partly about facts (was the person ignorant of important facts which could be expected to influence his choice if he had known them?) and partly about capacities (was he incapacitated in some relevant way from making an adequate appraisal of these facts and their bearing on his decision?).

This notion of incapacity is highly relevant, since many of the decisions made by social workers about other people's welfare rest on an appeal to the incapacity of those people to decide for themselves. The importance of these arguments is that they suggest very strongly that our criterion of 'incapacity to decide' cannot be based simply on the nature of the decision and our disagreement with it. If we wish to set the decision aside as reflecting a person's incapacity to assess his own welfare, we are arguing in a circle unless we have some *other* evidence of relevant incapacity. If my client makes a decision with which I disagree, I cannot regard him as incompetent to make that decision simply because I disagree with it; I would need some other evidence of characteristic disturbances of thought or emotion or other relevant incapacities which indicate a general difficulty in exercising rational preference. Otherwise I am making the same kind of mistake attributed to the stereotypical Freudian analyst who (allegedly) regards his patient's denial of illness as confirmation of illness since it indicates the persistence of his defences against recognising his condition. If a decision that I know what is good for somebody better than he knows it himself can be based simply on the fact that his conclusions differ from mine, there is no logical limit to my right to interfere 'for his own good', and nobody would logically be immune from my ministrations if he disagreed with me. Social workers who interpret their task in very positive terms such as the 'promotion of mental hygiene' seem particularly at risk in this way, and it is difficult not to prefer the traditional liberal doctrine that the burden of proving the necessity of interference rests on those who wish to interfere.

Of course the category of those who have limited competence to make decisions about their own welfare is quite wide: it includes, in many respects, young children, and in some respects the mentally ill and handicapped, the temporarily emotionally disturbed, and so on. However, in making decisions on behalf of such people we should, if we accept Brandt's arguments, be sure first that their competence is limited in respect of the particular decision involved, and a good way to avoid the over-estimation of incompetence might be to ensure maximum opportunities for people to be involved in decisions as far as they are able. If we can identify no relevant incapacities but still find it necessary to override clients' views, this should only be done in accordance with some general duty (for instance to protect the interests of others) and should not be misrepresented as a form of helping 'for their own good'.

A number of objections can be advanced against the kind of position summarised here, which is basically a traditional liberal view that a rational and well-informed person should be regarded as the best judge of his own interests even if our own preferences are different. This is essentially a subjectivist view of interests, and as such presents difficulties for arguments which analyse social situations in terms of collective interests (such as class interests) which are treated as having an objective status even if the members of that collective have not expressed them or are unaware of them. Although space precludes a detailed discussion of these arguments here, a few points are worth noting. For instance, an objective concept of 'interest' which differs from 'what people rationally prefer' allows us to point to the possibility that people may be influenced against 'their real interests' by ideologies in society which present certain goals as valuable when others might be more valuable. Various attempts have been made to reconcile the primacy of the individual's subjective judgements of interest with a more objective view of potential interest which might allow a critique of the way in which, in a particular society, people's views of their interests become distorted. Marcuse, for instance, attempts to distinguish between 'true' needs, which all people share, and 'false' needs which are ideologically manufactured by powerful social interests and constitute a form of repression (Marcuse 1964). Most Marxist writers similarly seek to distinguish between objective class interests and the 'false consciousness' which usually prevents working-class people from articulating what are taken to be their objective interests. Some problems associated with the notion of 'false consciousness' will be discussed later in connection with consciousness raising, but it is clear that most attempts to introduce the notion of 'objective interests' depend on assumptions about the interests which people would express and act upon if certain socially structured incapacities were removed. Thus Habermas (1976), for instance, suggests that people can arrive at rational choices through free argument between equals in the absence of ideological and political coercion, and Lukes (1974) argues that interests reflect the choices people would make under conditions of relative autonomy; thus these writers do not seem fundamentally to disagree with the notion that interests have something to do with preferences exercised under conditions that allow rational choice. The differences are mainly in the nature and extent of the obstacles to rationality which they identify, and in the degree of confidence shown by proponents of 'objective interests' in predicting the choices that people would make if free to do so. In these arguments they face problems which are similar to those involved in a social worker's decision made on behalf of an incapacitated person. Traditional liberal theory would argue that such decisions should take account of the preferences that person would be likely to have if not incapacitated, or perhaps the preferences that a reasonable person in those circumstances would have. For instance, Watson (1980) in a discussion of the ethics of behaviour modification argues that 'if this part of social welfare provision is to be seriously described as "help" and not to be regarded as a tool in social engineering, behaviour modification . . . must suit the patient's purposes', but these may not be easy to discern.

Saunders (1980), in a discussion of the attempts of urban sociologists to develop conceptions of the objective interests of social groups involved in urban social change, suggests another way around this problem — namely that, in certain contexts, we can assume by convention that certain objective interests are relevant, whether or not they are actually expressed. He uses the example of the effects of social change on health, and suggests that given a particular context such as health it makes sense to describe, for instance, clean air as being in people's real interests whether or not they express this preference themselves. However, health is perhaps one of the easiest contexts in which to do this since people characteristically prefer not to be ill and this provides a good basis for accommodation between imputed and expressed interests. Social workers are often involved in more complex situations where the possible courses of action are many and the effects on people's interests both diverse and unpredictable, and it would be difficult, particularly for adult clients, to generate a widely acceptable set of assumptions about objective interests on a basis of convention.

On the whole, then, however necessary some notion of objective interests may be as an analytical tool for understanding the role of ideology in forming conceptions of interest, social workers are necessarily more involved with the small-scale detail of how to promote individual welfare and personal interests in complex situations. Here the notion of objective interests, whether of the 'mental hygiene' variety, the 'true consciousness' variety or any other, involves serious risks since it encourages us to imagine that we already know what the client's problems are without having made an effort to elicit and understand his own subjective perception of them. It may be useful to have an underlying conception of common human needs, but not if it obstructs the appreciation of specific individual need.

A recent piece of research concerning social work in criminal justice provides an illustration of some of these difficulties (Raynor 1981). The study attempted to identify the personal and social difficulties reported by a group of 19 probationers attending the day training centre in Pontypridd and to compare these with assessments made by professionals at various stages of supervision. Its relevance to the issue of subjective and objective interests lies in the fact that probationers were encouraged as part of the assessment procedure at the centre to identify those problems which seemed to them to be areas of difficulty in their lives, through the use of comprehensive checklists (a version of the Mooney Problem Checklist) as an instrument for eliciting self-reported problems. This provides an indication of what they subjectively saw as the obstacles to their own interests, and part of the study involved comparing these client statements with the statements of welfare professionals (in this case, probation officers) who were involved in attributing problems to them. These attributions were made particularly in the social inquiry reports presented to the courts as background information when they were sentenced, and in follow-up assessments at a later stage of their probation orders some time after the completion of their required attendance at the centre.

Readers interested in the detailed evidence about how frequently different kinds of problems were mentioned by clients and professionals are referred to the original article, but several of the findings are of interest for our current purposes. For instance, clients and professionals did not agree particularly closely about the *extent* of their problems, and there were also some interesting differences in the *kinds* of problem identified. The five problem areas most often mentioned in the self-reports were, in order of frequency: employment; income; health; social relationships; and accommodation. In the social inquiry reports, the most frequent were: employment; family relationships; income; social relationships; and lack of motivation. The follow-up assessments attributed lack of motivation in every case, and the other frequent areas were family relationships; income; employment; and relationships with people in authority.

In other words, the clients were more inclined to give high priority to problems of basic practical resources (and also, incidentally, often identified far more problems than were mentioned in the social inquiry reports). The professional assessments were more likely to introduce issues concerning relationships and motivation, and often seemed not to be descriptive statements about areas of difficulty so much as interpretative statements about the *presumed reasons* for people having difficulties (e.g. lack of motivation). This is not to say they were necessarily 'incorrect'; the problem of evaluating the correctness of interpretative statements about other people's motivation is a major issue on its own, and not one into which I intend to enter here. Rather, the professional assessments were clearly drawn from professional training and professional frames of reference which were based on something other than what clients themselves identified as important, and reflected a judgement of 'objective interests' which may well be less accessible and useful to clients than their own assessment of their own problems. Such a conclusion is strongly suggested by Bottoms and McWilliams's (1979) arguments in favour of abandoning pretensions to 'diagnosis' and 'treatment' of offenders, and concentrating instead on the collaborative definition of problems and on help towards agreed goals.

So should we abandon all claims to expertise in understanding problems, and concentrate simply on the relief of 'presenting problems'? Here, I think, a note of caution is necessary. The choice is not simply between pseudo-medical diagnostic pretensions and a blind adherence to the first difficulty our client happens to mention. The fact that the men in this study were mostly able to produce comprehensive and useful assessments of their own problems and to contribute actively to the formulation of goals and programmes should not blind us to the fact that they had not done so before, although the problems were often of long standing. Their achievement reflects the provision of an appropriate context, practical and effective methods, and an atmosphere of encouragement, support and some demand. In other words, the clients' statements about their own interests were not produced in the absence of any influence at all. If social workers have skills in understanding problems, these may perhaps be more usefully understood as skills in helping people to arrive at their own understanding than as skills in making accurate diagnoses for professional use. But if 'respect for persons' implies respect for clients' free choices, what kinds of influence can we reasonably exercise to close the gap between subjective and objective assessment of clients' interests? To what extent, and in what circumstances, do influence and persuasion infringe respect for personal liberty and become a form of covert coercion? Here again we find ourselves in an area of conceptual difficulty.

FREEDOM AND INFLUENCE

From the argument so far, it is clear that one way of influencing decisions without infringing respect for personal choices is to try to make those choices more informed: in other words, to assist with the factual element in decisions about interests, rather than with the evaluative element. In the discussion of the 'sentenced to social work' approach to probation practice, the question was raised whether clients could make realistic choices which genuinely reflected an informed perception of their interests when faced with the possibility of using a number of different sources of help about which they knew very little. The general aim of allowing clients free choice about the kind of help they needed seemed likely to suffer through their lack of experience of what might be involved in making one choice rather than another. It is interesting that some probation teams which have attempted to put this model into practice have had to devise ways of helping clients to make informed choices, and that their methods go well beyond the original paper's suggestion of informative posters in the waiting room.

For instance, of the two teams in Hampshire whose attempts to operate this type of scheme were evaluated by the Home Office Research and Planning Unit, one developed the use of 'needs questionnaires' which probationers completed early in their orders and the other required each probationer to attend six 'induction group' sessions. These were designed to introduce the clients to the various resources and facilities available in the office before they decided whether to enter into a social work contract or to continue their order by reporting only. In both offices it appeared that sentencers were prepared to make this new type of probation order and that the rate of attendance of probationers at the offices was increased without an increase in breach proceedings, but there was little evidence that more standardised expectations of reporting and breach procedures made magistrates more likely to use probation as an alternative to custody (Smith et al. 1984). What is clear is that the probation officers felt it necessary to help their clients to make informed choices, and it is arguable that this model may be more consistent with 'respect for persons' than the model of virtually unaided choice suggested in the original paper (Bryant et al. 1978).

Another interesting example occurred in the day training centre involved in the study of problem attribution mentioned earlier in this chapter. The centre provides a variety of learning opportunities, from the mainly practical (such as the workshop) to the more personal and problem-centred (such as the social skills group). In keeping with the policy of involving clients in planning their programme, trainees are invited to select from a 'programme checklist' the things they would like to do and feel that they need to work on. After experimenting with the use of this checklist in a context of relatively unaided choice without much prior discussion, an induction group was introduced in which each member was encouraged to undertake a detailed assessment of himself, his situation, his offending, and his needs. The checklist was then completed after the induction group. Early impressions of the new procedure suggested that it increased clients' preparedness to opt for more personally challenging activities and to make fuller use of them (Vanstone forthcoming).

A sceptic might argue that such exercises, far from increasing the influence of clients' choices, could be simply a covert means of indoctrinating clients in the social worker's view of their problems; however, there is in practice a large difference between a dialogue based on genuine participation and a one-sided diagnostic exercise in which the client is treated as incompetent to decide for himself. Greater problems, perhaps, occur when discussion is not so much about what would be a helpful way of pursuing client goals as about whether those goals are desirable in themselves — in other words, about the normative component of welfare decisions.

An interesting paper by Benn (1967) concerns itself precisely with the question of when attempts to persuade people to take a different view of their interests amount to an infringement of their liberty. He suggests a number of criteria which might, in principle, help to distinguish those kinds of influence which enhance people's capacity for rational choice in their own interests from those kinds of influence which diminish the capacity to choose, and amount to a soft form of coercion. One of these is rationality: rational persuasion gives reasons, and is open to correction if better reasons can be found. Another is resistibility: if an influence is so strong, or so covertly insidious, that no one could reasonably be expected to resist it, it diminishes freedom. This suggests that social workers should be very careful to create opportunities for their clients to state their own views and if necessary to disagree, and that this needs to be a consistent feature of attempts to help rather than something which can be taken for granted after one instance of formal consent, such as the client's consent in court to the making of a probation order about which he may know very little.

Benn also considers the case of interference with someone 'for his own good', a discussion long overshadowed by J. S. Mill's classic statement:

> The sole end for which mankind . . . are warranted in interfering with the liberty of action of any of their number is self-protection. . . . The only purpose for which power can rightfully be exercised over any member of a civilised society, against his will, is to prevent harm to others. His own good is not a sufficient warrant. (Mill 1859)

While generally sympathetic to this point of view which, as noted earlier, places the burden of proof clearly on the shoulders of the would-be interferer, Benn argues that there are cases in which we can rightly intervene to prevent someone acting as he rationally chooses. These would be situations in which the chosen course of action would substantially limit the subject's *future* capacity to act in accordance with his rational choices — for instance, intervening to prevent a man deliberately addicting himself to a dangerous and disabling drug. Social workers will be familiar with situations of this general kind, and Benn's argument seems to suggest that if we interfere to prevent adverse consequences of freely chosen actions for the person concerned (leaving aside for a moment the important question of effects on others), and if that interference is to be consistent with respecting the person's liberty, then those adverse consequences would need to be certain rather than simply possible.

Overall, if we take this kind of argument seriously, it appears that probation officers and social workers who resist involvement in more coercive and directive policies on the grounds that it conflicts with their 'social work identity' are not necessarily being insubordinate, evasive, conservative or professionally precious. On the contrary, there are strong reasons to suggest that respect for persons and for their liberty, is, or should be, a fundamental feature of welfare services in any society which aspires to democracy. Respect for persons seems to require that interference be strictly limited to the minimum amount necessary, and that attempts to influence should rely not on one-sided processes like coercion or imposed diagnosis, but on two-sided participatory processes resembling negotiation and dialogue: 'Rational persuasion is . . . essentially a dialogue between equals' (Benn 1967). Two-sided processes involve a balance, an 'equilibration', which needs to be guarded carefully against the temptations of premature certainty. The next chapter considers some recent approaches to dialogue and negotiation which have sought to influence social work practice.

5

Negotiation, Dialogue and Problem-Solving

Respect for persons and respect for clients' choices, if taken seriously as a value base for social work practice, imply that attempts to influence those choices must involve elements of dialogue and negotiation. In other words, a model of typical processes of influence in social work would resemble at least a two-sided problem-solving process rather than a one-sided process of diagnosis and treatment. The idea of social work as essentially a problem-solving process is not, of course, new, and was elaborated nearly 30 years ago by Perlman (1957), but it is doubtful if its full potential and implications for social work with offenders have been explored, partly because the criminal justice system itself resists definition as a problem-solving institution. (Some of the possible applications of this perspective to criminal justice will be considered later.) For our present purposes, it is interesting to note that some recent writing about the place of dialogue and problem-solving in social change processes has been quite widely discussed in social work but seems on the whole not to have entered yet into the theoretical debates about the role of social workers in criminal justice.

CONSCIOUSNESS-RAISING AND LIBERATION

The most influential recent attempts to articulate the place of dialogical relationships (relationships based on mutual communication) in social work practice are found in accounts of 'radical' social work informed by Paulo Freire's concept of 'conscientization' or consciousness-raising. In its origins as an educational technique used among illiterate and politically oppressed social groups in Latin America, 'conscientization' was a process which sought to combine basic educational aims with the development of a 'critical consciousness' which could understand and, potentially, transform the political culture of oppressive social systems (Freire 1972). Traditional education, a one-way process of transferring knowledge from high-status experts to inferiors who were presumed ignorant, was contrasted with a more democratic model of mutual education through dialogue in which educators would help people to develop the tools to understand in a more critical way the reality they already experienced, and would at the same time learn from them through confrontation with this experience. The learner's consciousness was seen not as empty, waiting to be filled by the educator, but as oppressed by ignorance, ideology or conventional education, and capable of original and creative responses through being 'raised' to a level of critical reflection on experience. In this way processes of education, help and political mobilisation against oppressive social realities could be and needed to be combined.

This approach to education had an immediate influence on progressive social workers in Latin America, and began to have a substantial influence on social and community work in industrialised Europe in the early 1970s. At the sixteenth International Congress of Schools of Social Work in Holland in 1972 Luis Alfero, a Chilean social work educator, presented a paper entitled 'Conscientization'. This was widely quoted and quickly recognised as relevant by European radical social workers who found their colleagues in Latin America expressing, through their professional organisations, an explicit link between the aims of social work and the process of political change. For instance, a Latin American Seminar of Schools of

Social Work in Ecuador in 1971 concluded that 'Social work will be able to contribute to the transformation of the present situation only so long as it commits itself to man and society in the social change process. Social work implies talking in terms of a reflexive, horizontal, dynamic communication which will dialectically feed back into action' (Alfero 1972).

This explicit linking of critical understanding with liberating action ('praxis') had an obvious appeal for social workers impatient with an individualised 'treatment' model which seemed to concentrate on diagnostic understanding at the expense of action. A number of social and community workers took up the idea of 'conscientization' and applied it to their own work; Peter Leonard is a typical example, in his adoption of 'conscientization' as one of the elements for the construction of a paradigm of radical social work practice. Social workers could, he suggests, help their clients to free themselves from oppressed and fragmented consciousness and to develop a critical consciousness of their own oppression and their own potential for bringing about change. Such perspectives provided a clear alternative to the policy of 'blaming the victim' or encouraging the poor to feel responsible for and guilty about their poverty. They also seemed to offer an escape from one-sided diagnosis and the authority of the helper: 'radical change can only come from consciousness developed as a result of exchange rather than imposition' (Leonard 1975). Whether or not this is empirically true, it seems to outline an ethical stance which respects clients' choices and allows their perceptions and views a high degree of validity.

Other commentators on Freire have, however, seriously questioned the apparent egalitarianism of this model of consciousness-raising. Gleeson (1974), for instance, asks 'What does he mean by 'authentic', 'true' or 'real' consciousness? . . . How can Freire be sure that conscientised revolutionaries will not become oppressors themselves?' The central problem is that if we set out to raise someone else's consciousness, this implies that we know the difference between higher and lower states of consciousness, which in turn implies that we know in advance something about what a raised consciousness is like. This begins to look (despite dialogue, egalitarianism and so on) alarmingly like traditional one-sided diagnosis — the helper knows what is wrong with the client even if the client does not, and the fact that the client does not know represents 'false consciousness' which in turn confirms the diagnosis. In practice, there is an ever-present danger that raising someone's consciousness simply means getting the client to see the world as the helper sees it — in other words, a form of indoctrination.

Although it can be reasonably argued that some forms of consciousness or cognitive capacity are higher, or more capable, than others, when such arguments are convincing they rest on fairly obvious objective differences, as between adults and small children. When adults disagree, it is far more difficult to find an objective yardstick to measure the level of consciousness. Peter Berger (1976) states the problem more dramatically: 'It is, in principle, impossible to "raise the consciousness" of anyone, because all of us are stumbling around on the same level of consciousness — a pretty dim level. . . . If the concept of 'consciousness-raising' has any merit, we would recommend that it be employed for any enterprise that teaches a consciousness of limits.' The message seems to be that social workers, in embracing the function of consciousness-raising, may be departing less than they think from their traditional function of knowing better than other people; superior insight has simply acquired a radical gloss.

As a corrective against these dangers, Berger suggests the principle of 'cognitive respect': that is, we should start from the assumption that each man is normally the expert on his own situation, and that while consciousnesses may differ we should beware of arranging them in a hierarchy of value, with some regarded as better than others. He also points out that from a sociological point of view 'consciousness raising' is mostly done by upper-class intellectuals to lower-class target groups and that it should be recognised as a process of influence rather than a vehicle of participation, which requires a more respectful and less dismissive approach to the views of the participating actors.

BEYOND THE ZERO-SUM GAME

One writer who has attempted to spell out the basis of a problem-solving dialogue which does not start from an assumption of 'higher consciousness' on the helper's part is John Burton, originally a specialist in diplomacy and international relations who become interested in the potential contribution of non-coercive solutions to political and social conflicts. His ideas are set out mainly in two books (Burton 1969 and 1979) which aim to indicate some general features of successful problem-solving processes which tend to exist regardless of the size of the system in which the conflict occurs, whether between nations, between individuals, or between deviants and social control systems.

The starting-point of this general model of problem-solving processes is that in all human conflict the perception, interpretations and assumptions of actors are of central importance, since these determine the value placed on whatever the conflict is about and the meanings attributed to the actions of other parties. Although some conflicts may have an objective basis, for instance in the scarcity of some resource needed by both parties, the obstacles to resolution are usually partly subjective. In particular, both parties typically assume that all possible outcomes are 'zero-sum': in other words, that one party's gain must be the other's loss. From such a position they are likely to move either to escalated conflict or to the coercive imposition of an apparent solution by the exercise of power, which itself expends scarce resources and creates new sources of conflict. In Burton's view, much conventional thinking about social and political problems contributes to this kind of failure to resolve problems effectively because theorists have concentrated too much on the needs for stability and continuity in social systems and not enough on the process of adaptation and response to change. This one-sided view has encouraged us to approach problems by trying to coerce or 'resocialize' deviant individuals, groups or nations into conformity with system demands, often with little constructive effect. Problems may be temporarily contained or repressed in this way (as in an efficient police state) or they may be aggravated (as when deviant identities and behaviour are confirmed by attempts at correction), but they are not solved. Burton's interest is therefore in problem-solving procedures which rely neither on compulsion nor on the unreliable assumption that the parties already share a consensus about basic values. He asks 'under what conditions and by what processes can there be a harmonious and co-operative society despite the absence both of shared values and of coercion?'

Sweeping questions like this are, of course, notoriously difficult to answer meaningfully; however, at the everyday level of participation in small-scale social systems it does seem possible to identify some alternatives to zero-sum conflicts. Burton argues that participants in systems typically seek satisfaction of certain basic needs, including non-material needs for recognition, for identity, for participation in decisions and for a degree of control or influence over the operation of systems. Needs of this kind may often be met by non-material social goods (such as identity, recognition and so on) which are elastic, in the sense that their supply is not necessarily restricted by material scarcity and they do not therefore require to be distributed on a zero-sum basis. Some interactions increase the sum of non-material goods for all parties, for instance when mutual respect is established.

Burton's attempt to delineate basic human needs has parallels in the work of a number of other writers (for instance Maslow 1954, or Kellmer Pringle 1974 on the needs of children), but his particular interest for a discussion of conflict and control lies in his argument that members of systems are often restrained from overtly conflictual behaviour neither by shared values nor by coercion, but by functional transactions with other members which meet needs. This suggests that our ways of handling conflicts, particularly conflicts involving relatively small systems and few contending parties, should seek to meet the needs of all parties and should not assume a zero-sum, win-or-lose outcome. For instance, if all parties emerge feeling that they have been recognised, understood, valued, taken seriously and treated with respect, this may be a relatively satisfactory outcome for all, without the need to attribute 'false consciousness' to anyone.

This type of argument suggests particular approaches to the problem-solving activity of helping other parties to manage their conflicts with each other, and it is here that Burton's ideas come closest to the concerns of social work. For instance, he suggests that helping conflicting parties requires a 'no-fault' or non-judgemental orientation, in which the concern is not to allocate blame but to ensure that both parties become better informed about each other's needs, motives, aspirations and perceptions of the current predicament. This increases the opportunities for each to re-examine assumptions in the light of new knowledge about the other. The goal is to assist the parties, with information and possible options, to choose their own solutions rather than having solutions imposed on them, and the process aims to allow both parties to feel recognized and able to exercise some control. If the process 'works', both parties can feel reasonably satisfied with an outcome which reduces problems for both, and the satisfaction of parties can be used as a non-Utopian criterion of improvement. If it does not work, the parties can revert to their own previous styles of conflict without having lost very much. (Nor is it suggested that this kind

of approach to problem-solving can resolve *all* conflicts
— simply that its use may create more opportunities for
the management of conflict by agreement rather than by
coercive violence.)

This type of conflict-management through negotiation,
with its concern for dialogue and understanding, combines
an awareness of the importance of communication with a
traditional emphasis on respect and insight. What is seen
as effective communication from the point of view of the
system as a whole is experienced by individual parties as
new understanding of others or of themselves. Thus occurs
an interesting convergence between different strands of
social work: the more recent, sociologically influenced
emphasis on understanding systems of social interaction
and influencing the nature and quality of transactions
within them (e.g. Pincus and Minahan 1973) turns out to
require behaviour from the helper which is very similar to
earlier prescriptions for 'non-directive' helping. Research
in psychotherapy has consistently pointed to the helpful
effects of accurate empathy: that is, accurate understanding
of the client's experience which is communicated back to
him and adds to his own understanding (Truax and
Carkhuff 1967, Sutton 1979). The same is true of what
American therapists have called 'warmth', some researchers
'unconditional positive regard' and British textbooks, with
characteristic reserve, 'respect' or 'concern' — that is, the
communication of a positive concern without possessive-
ness, incorporation or 'taking-over'. Similarly, 'concrete-
ness' (clarity and specificity of communication as opposed
to vagueness and abstraction) and 'genuineness' (authen-
ticity, credibility) have stood up well in research and
practice as components of successful helping, and would
seem equally relevant to the task of promoting constructive exchange between parties in Burton's model of
conflict-management.

Thus the attempt to identify models of helping which
give adequate weight to the need for dialogue and
negotiation in situations of conflict between authorities

and subjects leads ironically in a full circle towards some traditional features of Rogerian non-directive counselling — the same tradition of voluntary therapeutic contact which led psychiatric social workers of the early sixties to regard probation work as 'not really social work' because of its compulsory elements. The non-directive therapists, however, were concerned primarily about the two-party relationship between client (or patient) and therapist, and their concern that important decisions should be made as far as possible by the client implied, primarily, that they should not be made for him by the therapist. When they saw probation officers telling their clients that they should do this or that and refrain from doing something else, they saw this as a similar two-party relationship in which the probation officer was directing instead of helping, and probation officers responded by arguing that this direction was in fact a form of help because it corresponded to what clients really needed.

It is a central part of the argument of this book that both parties in this old controversy were mistaken. Although there may well have been plenty of examples of inappropriate coerciveness by probation officers, the view that this is somehow inherent in their role depends on a misreading of the probation relationship as a transaction between only two parties, in which one makes demands and the other complies or rebels. In fact, both officer and client are part of a far wider pattern of transactions and contracts. Perhaps the most important contribution of the social sciences to social work practice is to remind us that social work is typically not a private and protected two-party transaction between helper and helped but is inextricably involved in a wider system of social processes, which usually have something to do with managing the needy or the deviant. The role of the probation officer or social worker in criminal justice can be more fruitfully understood as that of a negotiator or mediator in the decision-making system rather than a decision-maker or source of coercive authority in his own right.

Two examples from related fields may help to clarify the distinction. Leonard (1976) suggests that much everyday social work has a 'mediating' function in that social workers become involved in the interaction between individual clients and the institutions that control needed resources or exercise power. The social worker's job is then to promote effective communication and perhaps some mutual adaptation to secure a positive outcome for the client (and, if we abandon the zero-sum assumptions of crude conflict models, presumably on occasion a positive outcome for the institution too). Thus the client who is being deprived of supplementary benefit by an inefficient, prejudiced or overloaded bureaucracy may be helped to apply pressure to change the agency's response to his needs and may also be encouraged to present his claim in a more technically convincing and effective way, thus going some way towards adapting his own behaviour to the requirements of the agency. This is very clearly a three-party transaction, not one in which the client is made to change his behaviour simply to meet the social worker's requirements. Nor is it the social worker who is failing to respond to the client's claim. And yet the partly analogous three-party transaction of court, supervisor and client is often treated as a two-party relationship in which the supervisor, rather than the court, is seen as the source of the demands made on the client.

The second example is drawn from Benn's discussion of the problems surrounding the concepts of freedom and persuasion in moral philosophy. In the course of developing this argument that rational persuasion does not infringe autonomy, he makes the following point:

> Of course, not any kind of reason will do. To give as a reason the injury you will do to me if I reject your suggestion is to threaten me, not to use rational persuasion. However, some neutral or disinterested person with no control over your behaviour would

be using rational persuasion if *he* warned me of what you would do to me if I disobeyed you. (Benn 1967)

The implication is that if you warn me of probable coercive intervention by some third party, you are not yourself acting coercively towards me, but rather helpfully in making me aware of a relevant fact about my circumstances.

Thus a model of problem-solving by non-coercive negotiation can allow not only an appreciation of the conflicting perceptions and expectations of parties but also a recognition of the constraints and limits which are imposed by the non-negotiable aspects of the situation or by the probable behaviour of other parties. A framework of this kind can incorporate and recognise both the importance of individual choice and the reality of social controls or system constraints, and suggests a process in which their competing claims can be explored and tested.

However, unfortunately for the clarity and simplicity to which moral philosophers aspire, the real life of a probation officer is not as tidy as Benn's example. Sometimes, certainly, he may be in the situation of exploring options with the client on the basis of what actions a third party, the court, might take; but on other occasions he may be directly involved in trying to influence the court, or conversely making directive demands himself on the client. Although these directive powers may be delegated from the court, he can exercise them within limits on his own initiative, and is then not (in Benn's terms) a 'neutral or disinterested person with no control over your behaviour'. As well as trying to influence or help their clients, probation officers and social workers often make demands on them, and any account of the function of social work in criminal justice must reflect the reality of making demands as well as of helping. It is not enough to argue, with Day (1983), that most clients expect direction and that care and control thereby become compatible. Although care often involves control, it is abundantly clear that not all control is caring, and the problem is to elucidate when, and in what circumstances, directive demands should be made and controls exercised within a model that stresses negotiation and non-coercive problem-solving. To begin to explore this, it is necessary to re-examine the successes and failures of some earlier attempts to clarify the issue of directive authority in social work.

6

Social Work and Social Control: Choice and Constraint

When social workers or probation officers exercise directive powers over their delinquent clients, sometimes this is as an agent of a third party (a court or the Home Office) enforcing rules about which the individual social worker has little or no choice. At other times, the social worker or probation officer himself has the discretion to exercise directive or coercive powers. Traditional discussions of the probation officer's 'authority' make few distinctions between these two situations, tending to see authority in the supervisory relationship as undivided and deriving mainly from the officer. In reality, the distinction is important not only morally (as in Benn's example in the previous chapter) but practically in terms of the kind of demand which can reasonably be made on clients. Where the probation officer is simply an instrument (willing or unwilling) of directive requirements laid down by a court, the coercive nature of his actions needs to be considered as one example of the function of control and coercion in the wider criminal justice system. The coerciveness of criminal justice and the coerciveness of social work with offenders are of course linked, and changes in one can affect the other: some aspects of these links are explored in later chapters. However, when the probation officer or social worker decides, on his own initiative, that control and direction are required, this individual decision requires a different kind of justification.

The type of justification for control which is offered by 'treatment' models is again best represented by the work of Foren and Bailey (1968). In their sustained attempt to justify the use of control for probationers' 'own good' they try to distinguish between oppressive and benign authority, and introduce the notion of 'assertive casework' based on benign authority. This they believe to be similar to the normal processes of social control which shape our social behaviour as we progress from infancy to 'mature' self-direction, and they depend heavily on an analogy with parents' authority over children, suggesting that the extra element of social work supervision is brought into play by a court when these 'natural' processes have broken down. In other words, 'immature' people are not expected to be self-directing, and need to be controlled if they are to develop towards self-direction. The major difficulty for Foren and Bailey's argument is that they fail to produce any convincing criteria of 'maturity' other than conformity with society's norms, as if there were no distinctions to be drawn between individual interests and the enforcement of other people's expectations. The arguments reviewed in previous chapters suggest that this is both philosophically unsound and sociologically unrealistic. The philosophical error lies in interpreting non-conformity (or disagreement) as evidence of the kind of incapacity which would justify the imposition of someone else's judgements about the client's welfare; as we have seen, such interference needs to be justified by other evidence of relevant incapacities, not simply by the fact of disagreement. Sociologically, the notion that non-conformity can be equated with deficient socialisation assumes a degree of consensus and community of values which is not characteristic of the kind of society in which social workers are typically employed. Again Becker summarises the problem neatly:

It is harder in practice than it appears to be in theory to specify what is functional or dysfunctional for a society or a social group. . . . Factions within the group disagree and manoeuvre to have their own definition of the group's function accepted. The function of the group or organisation, then, is decided in political conflict, not given in the nature of the organisation. (Becker 1963)

Social workers in modern industrial societies seem, in fact, typically to operate at points of contradiction and potential conflict in social systems and are presented daily with discrepancies between individual needs and available resources, between welfare and economic utility, between social rights and structural inequalities, or between humanistic and instrumental approaches to the value of persons. To seek guidance from an established consensus in such areas will often be impossible.

Nor is it persuasive to argue that because social control is a necessary feature of shared experience in any society it therefore requires no further justification as a legitimate activity for social workers. Of course social life requires social control: the process of socialisation, of shaping behaviour and learning the shared meanings which make social interaction and communication possible, involves controls which limit the potential variety and diversity of behaviour. A similar point was made in considering 'respect for persons' as a necessary condition of communication. It can also be argued that freedom presupposes order: in other words, our capacity to choose how to act depends on being able to know something about the probable consequences of our actions, and this requires a context which is to some extent ordered and predictable. If the consequences of acts are random, there are no reasons for preferring one course of action over another. In societies which are exposed to massive social disruption, normal social behaviour and co-operation can break down completely, producing an unstable collection of individual predators and isolates, inhuman because they are asocial. This process has been documented, for instance by Colin Turnbull (1973) in his account of the disintegration of the Ik, a forcibly transplanted African tribe. However, such evidence of the interdependence of social action and social control falls a long way short of demonstrating that all non-conformity provides a legitimate occasion for interference by coercive experts. If one necessary condition of liberty is freedom from arbitrary and unpredictable interference by others, this also implies freedom from arbitrary interference by the State, and it is a commonplace of democratic political theory that the State's right to interfere with individuals should be limited by laws which define what are and are not grounds for interference. Social workers in the criminal justice system are typically State employees and their powers should be correspondingly limited. To return to Turnbull's study, it is interesting to note that the destruction of the tribe's social organisation and culture was in fact initiated by coercive government measures. In short, the evidence that social control is a necessary part of social life does not support the coercive or paternalistic exercise of official control over non-conforming citizens. Societies can tolerate a high degree of pluralism and diversity, and may in fact increase their adaptability by doing so, but living with diversity requires effective arrangements for communicating and managing differences. As in Rex's 'social system of the truce', social order need not presuppose consensus of values and interests provided there is some agreement about the scope, mechanisms and rules of conflict (Rex 1961).

These considerations direct our attention to a limited area of consensus which has some relevance to the social worker's right to intervene. In chapter 4 it was suggested that one reason for overriding people's preferences, or interfering with their freedom, could be the threat posed by their behaviour to others, though such overriding is correctly identified as 'control' rather than 'help'. One aspect of the partial commitment to welfare in modern industrial societies is the emergence, through the political process, of widespread agreement that certain groups of citizens are ill equipped to fend for themselves and require special resources and services — for instance, children, sick people, the disabled, the elderly, the mentally ill. There have also been successful demands that the State provide resources for some groups who would otherwise be disadvantaged by the unrestricted pursuit of economic utility. Such State provision is often equivocal about whether it is conferring benefits or providing controls, and often reflects ambiguity of political purpose by imposing duties on welfare agencies without providing the resources to finance them adequately. Also, social policies developed in a context of very unequally distributed wealth and power often create categories of people who are treated *as if* they are incapable of perceiving their own interests, and need therefore to be subject to paternalistic regulation and control by social welfare services, when their real difficulties arise not from incapacity but from an imposed restriction of opportunities. For instance, old, sick or unemployed people who are also poor, powerless and dependent on the State for basic resources will often be treated as if they are incapable of deciding for themselves what they need, when similar people who are not poor, and can therefore purchase services, will be treated quite differently and with more respect. This has more to do with the imposition of stigma on those unable to participate in the free market than with helping people to pursue their legitimate interests. Social workers may often be expected to collude in paternalistic regulation of the poor when they might serve their clients better by helping them to overcome some of the restrictions imposed on them; however, there remain many areas of State provision which represent a more genuine commitment to social welfare, and where social workers can turn to legislation or explicit policy as representing a more widely agreed legitimation of their right to intervene.

For instance, the freedom of parents to batter their children is restricted in the interests of the children, and most people agree that it should be. Similarly, most people agree that their property should be safe from arbitrary interference and themselves from arbitrary assault, and there is broad support for the existence of social controls through a common criminal justice system even if many of its details are subject to dispute. Social workers within such a system draw their authority from the legitimacy generally accorded to the system and from political decisions that certain kinds of people need help, or that certain kinds of harm need to be prevented, in the general interest. To this extent social workers are not autonomous professionals deciding for themselves where they should become involved, where they should be directive or where they should interfere; the limits are set for them by law or policy or agency function rather than by such subtleties as the 'immaturity' of their clients. To return to Foren and Bailey, the probation officer's entitlement to expect his client to comply with certain rules does not arise from the officer's decision, in a two-party relationship, that his client requires direction because he is 'immature'. It arises instead from the decision by a third party, the court, that the probationer's freedom should be restricted as a consequence of his offences.

Such a decision does not imply any judgements about immaturity or incapacity for self-direction; it seeks instead to impose restrictions on behaviour, enforcing limits which are presumed to be in the general interest. In other words, while the authority to help lies with the client, who may or may not agree to engage in a co-operative problem-solving effort with his probation officer, the authority to make demands and to direct generally derives from, and is limited by, the sentencing court rather than the individual judgement of the officer. Thus the argument that offenders should be controlled in the interests of others provides a rationale for the court's control over offenders, and for directive action by social workers when they are acting as vehicles for the court's instructions; however, it does not provide a ready justification for the imposition of additional discretionary controls, even on the 'immature', which have not been required by the court nor agreed by the client.

Two further issues need consideration at this point. First, is it not the case that people *do* differ in social skills, in attainments, in socialisation, in capacity to make informed choices, and in many other ways? Could this not give some useful content to Foren and Bailey's concept of 'maturity' and their argument that clients of differing 'maturity levels' require different amounts of coercion from their supervisors? However, it is by no means clear that people can be reliably assigned to different categories of social competence or interpersonal maturity. Even the more highly developed systems of this kind, such as the 'I-level' categories used in the California Community Treatment Project, can produce agreement rates as low as 56 per cent when independently applied by two researchers to the same client population (Hood and Sparks, 1970, c. 7). In any case the idea that offenders who have committed similar offences could receive what are in effect different sentences because of personality or socialisation differences is difficult to reconcile with our conventional views about justice, and some problems of this kind are considered in the next chapter. A further difficulty is suggested by the earlier discussion of 'labelling': assignment to a category implying limited competence will tend to shape people's expectations and make it difficult to achieve transfer to a different category, even within a treatment regime which is intended to increase 'interpersonal maturity' or whatever other characteristic forms the basis of the classification. Such classifications are perhaps more appropriately used as an approximate guide to the range and type of facilities and programmes which a supervising agency might offer to its clients, rather than as a 'scientific' basis for differential sentencing.

A second and perhaps more important issue is raised by the emphasis placed throughout the last three chapters on client choice and on the element of voluntarism in helping, even where help is offered within the framework of a sentence determined by a court. It is often argued that choices offered in such circumstances are meaningless or a pure formality: for instance, consent in court to the making of a probation order may be given in ignorance of the alternatives or because it seems to be expected, and it is well established that many defendants neither understand nor feel involved in the majority of the proceedings in their own case (Carlen 1976). It is also sometimes suggested that consent to probation is unreal because the offender believes the alternative may be worse, and this is taken to mean that he is *really* being compelled even though he *appears* to be making a choice. This is a curious argument, since it implies that choices are not really free if one alternative seems preferable to the other, which is precisely what choices are about. In other words, choices made under the constraint of circumstances are nevertheless real choices, and the constraint arises simply from the fact that choices have consequences: the consequences of one alternative will be different from those of the other. In any situation short of total coercive control the element of choice remains, and the influences on that choice are constraints rather than compulsions. We can try to influence people's choices by persuasion or by attaching sanctions or rewards to one or other outcome, but the attempt to influence does not negate or abolish the fact of choice. Constraints or controls imposed for the benefit of persons other than the client may be necessary, but their nature and purpose should be explicit and not presented in a mystifying or mystified way, such as 'it's for your own good'. It was argued earlier that 'respect for persons' implies that one objective of social work should be to increase people's sense of identity and responsibility by increasing the range of situations in which they have a real choice of how to behave and how to realise their goals. This in turn suggests that social workers should try to find ways to make their clients' choices more informed and more real, confirming a sense of identity and responsibility rather than undermining it.

Bottoms and McWilliams (1979) have rightly pointed out that in some circumstances offenders are offered choices between alternatives both of which 'respect the individual so little as to amount to a form of coercion': their example is the practice in some countries of offering sex offenders a choice between indefinite imprisonment and castration. The problem here is not that they have no choice, but that both options are highly coercive and irreversible, like the choice traditionally offered by highwaymen to their victims: 'your money or your life.' The existence of some choice here does not negate the high level of coercion involved; however, the choices, constraints and influences operating in the context of social work with offenders cannot normally be of this character, since supervision in the open community inevitably limits the coercive apparatus available. The real nature of the choices imposed on, or available to, offenders and their supervisors are best illustrated by considering some practical examples.

The first concerns S, who first came to the probation officer's attention when he appeared in court for causing a disturbance at his estranged wife's temporary home. She had left him and several of their children following many years of rows. He was a large man in his forties with a loud voice, and a very threatening manner when he thought people were refusing to listen or to take him seriously. Old files revealed a childhood in local authority care and a history of offences as a young man, some violent, but none since his older children were born. Somebody somewhere had diagnosed him as an 'aggressive psychopath', and the files showed this label had stuck, in that professionals tended to disbelieve him and to treat him as dangerous. He had been to the social services for help in looking after his children and, probably, hoping for some support in persuading his wife to return, and he had been told that he should put the children into care and get a job despite being registered disabled through an industrial accident. By the time he came to court his relations with social security were as strained as his relations with the social services. The supplementary benefit officers tended to avoid contact with him and seemed to regard him as workshy, implying that he kept his children simply to increase his allowance, and social workers called infrequently and left quickly, sometimes after angry scenes in which S accused them of not being interested. He even claimed that some would push messages through the door and drive off rather than discuss matters with him. He himself had a keen sense of his rights and would quickly become very angry if he thought he was being 'messed around'. He threatened to defend his home violently if social workers came to remove his children, and he did not endear himself by his habit of turning up at various social work agencies in a tense and angry state demanding emergency assistance at inconvenient times. Thus his attempts to seek help tended to confirm his various labels and made it less likely that he would receive any. One social worker suggested that the most appropriate form of help for him would be regular visits from two or three very large policemen threatening to arrest him if he caused any trouble.

By the time he came to court he was a very frustrated man but spoke intelligently in his own defence, pointing out his concern to provide a home for his children and the difficulty he was having in coping without his wife. He recognised that he had lost his temper but indicated he would be prepared to co-operate with anyone who would try to help. In due course, following a social inquiry which confirmed that conditions for the children were tolerable and that he was making serious efforts at home, a probation order was made. The magistrates were clearly concerned about the potentially explosive situation and had probably been considering a custodial sentence to contain it, but they were pleased to be able to offer some help if there seemed to be a realistic prospect that something could be done.

The probation order started uneasily — S took to visiting the office every day with angry tales of the unfair way he was being treated, and tried hard to involve probation staff in a series of unrealistic manoeuvres to secure his wife's return; he also threatened staff and sometimes created a frightening sense of impending physical danger. After a few weeks of this, when it was clear that little progress was being made, a more planned approach was adopted which began by pointing out explicitly that the current situation met neither the letter nor the spirit of the probation order and was simply reproducing the problems he had experienced in seeking help from other agencies. Instead, the following principles were adopted, with S's rather guarded agreement: first, that a number of his difficulties arose from official views of him as an incompetent and dangerous nuisance, and his resentment of this led him to behave in ways which reinforced it. If he wanted to shed the label he needed to adopt a different and more rational pattern of problem-solving, including making appointments, *not* losing his temper (which never achieved anything anyway), and not deliberately manufacturing emergencies to put pressure on people. In short, he was not taken seriously because people assumed that he was incapable of acting in his own best interests, and since he claimed the right to be taken seriously (a right with which the probation officer sympathised) he needed to demonstrate the capacity and competence which people claimed he lacked.

The officer would guarantee availability at a fixed time each week to review the problem-solving efforts of the previous week and help to plan responses to the forseeable problems of the next week; he would also act as a mediator with some other agencies and support S's claims for fair treatment provided S handled the relevant encounters in the agreed way. Unplanned contacts were for genuine emergencies only, and the officer reserved the right to refuse to help with 'manufactured' emergencies. It was also agreed that if there was no serious attempt to adhere to these plans then this would call the whole basis of the probation order into question and must lead either to a different set of agreements or to a return to court on the basis that probation was impractical.

This was not, of course, a recipe for a trouble-free order; there were still a number of disagreements and conflicts — the real difficulties of S's situation presented a continuing challenge — the officer's advice sometimes turned out wrong and S's control over his temper would still occasionally slip. However, real and sustained progress was made in stabilising his life and establishing his right to reasonable treatment, and other agencies moved quite quickly from an initial scepticism (during which it was suggested that his improved behaviour was a 'manipulative' attempt to trick the probation officer into supporting him!) to a preparedness to co-operate. Interviews with the probation officer ceased to be used solely for threats and ventilation and became (mostly) problem-focused discussions where strategies for dealing with real difficulties could be explored and rehearsed in a friendly and co-operative way. When the officer behaved directively in insisting on planned appointments or refusing to respond to 'emergency' telephone calls, this was grudgingly accepted as appropriate to the agreed plan and did not precipitate any disasters, though the officer sometimes had to contain a good deal of anxiety after being told something like 'I'm going to set fire to all my furniture unless you do something straight away' and answering 'I know you feel like doing that, but if you actually do it, that's your choice and the consequences are your responsibility.'

This account illustrates a number of the themes which have been considered in this chapter. By offering to S the opportunity to demonstrate competence, the probation officer was also offering an opportunity to validate S's own understanding of his situation and its problems. By being seen to take responsibility, S could help to redefine his own 'case' in the eyes of agencies which had failed to help him because they assumed that he could not be helped. By making specific agreements which emphasized what each party would undertake to do, S and his probation officer were able to co-operate on a basis of mutual respect despite the unequal statutory relationship between them — a feature also noticed in the rather similar experimental attempts to practice task-centred casework within the framework of a probation order (Goldberg and Stanley 1979).

In terms of the argument of this chapter, S was not coerced but was involved in two sets of agreements, one with the court about the basic terms of the order and one with his officer about how those terms were to be interpreted and acted on. Both sets of agreements were revocable but neither was revocable without consequences, so both involved constraints. There were in fact a number of explicit discussions, at times when things were particularly difficult or prospects looked unusually gloomy, about the pros and cons of abandoning the probation order and asking the court to do something else, but in the event both parties decided each time that it was worth continuing. When the officer behaved directively, this was always in the context of prior agreements and took the form of insisting that if agreements were not adhered to they must either be renegotiated or explicitly broken, with all the consequences that would follow from this. The relationship was not free from attempts to influence (on both sides!) but it was intended to be as free as possible from deception and covert coercion.

This case provides one example of the use of explicit negotiation in a context of constraint within the framework of a probation order. It will be clear that 'social control' was recognised as an important objective by all three parties: the probation officer, the client and the court. However, it was not achieved by coercion, but by accepting the client's offer to assume control of his own affairs and behaviour and helping him to do this. His attempt to exercise control and responsibility was difficult for him, and would probably have not been made if he had not found himself in trouble, but he became an active partner in the search for solutions rather than a passive recipient of the probation officer's 'treatment'.

A somewhat similar example, this time a semi-fictional amalgam of cases developed for use in role-play exercises on confrontation skills, concerns problems of choice and constraint in the context of parole. A man on parole from a six-year prison sentence imposed for sexual assaults on children reports to his probation officer in an angry and agitated state. He has done well in securing accommodation and a job; however, his parole is conditional on co-operating with medical treatment which takes the form of daily doses of drugs. These reduce his sexual drive but also produce other unpleasant side-effects. He is frightened of prison, where he had a very bad time because of the nature of his offences, but he has come to tell his probation officer that he cannot take the drugs any more. His psychiatrist, who is not very sympathetic towards this type of offender, insists that the drugs are essential and 'do not usually' have side-effects. The officer knows that if his client stops taking the drugs he must report this to the Home Office, which is likely to lead to a recall to prison.

The difficulties of such an interview can safely be left to the reader's imagination; however it is interesting that the most convincing responses seem to be those that combine a clear empathic exploration and awareness of the client's predicament with an explicit explanation of the action the 'officer' is obliged to take, the reasons for it and the alternatives open to the 'client'. It seems important that the officer takes responsibility for his own part in the process rather than attributing all the blame to absent third parties such as the Home Office, since the client usually experiences this as evasive and frustrating. Sometimes the exercise ends with a joint agreement to reopen negotiations with the doctor to explore whether there are any alternative possibilities for medication. The principle, again, is to recognise the reality of all the constraints and difficulties while exploring those choices which remain open and their probable consequences, not as a cold intellectual exercise but as a shared attempt to confront real problems.

To return to the issues raised at the beginning of the chapter, I am suggesting by these arguments and examples that the probation officer's discretion to direct and to work assertively does not arise from the 'immaturity' of his clients nor from his expertise in devising 'treatments' for the objects of his supervision. I have argued instead that overtly directive work should occur in the context of explicit agreements and should reflect the need to ensure that these are not broken without a clear awareness of the consequences, including the legal and other constraints which created the original context of agreement. Courts can legitimately interfere with the liberty of offenders not because they are 'immature' but because they have been convicted of offences; probation officers and social workers can make demands on offenders within the context of a court order not because offenders are inherently incapable of self-direction but because, and only in so far as, the nature and scope of the demands have been agreed in advance. Such principles are consistent with moral assumptions about respect for persons and the importance of clients' choices. They also reinforce the suggestion that social workers and probation officers should try to ensure through negotiation and dialogue that clients' decisions to agree to certain kinds of demand are informed and realistic.

At this point it becomes necessary to consider how far the criminal justice system itself facilitates such principles. Does it provide a good context and a clear decision-making framework for a problem-solving approach to crime? Here again our two examples are interesting. S wanted to be on probation and consented to it willingly after some discussion at the social inquiry stage, but neither he nor his officer knew what alternative sentence the court had in mind to impose if he had not consented. (Both could make an informed guess, but that is not the point.) Similarly, our fictional parolee had chosen to apply for parole, but without knowing the grounds for granting or withholding it (which it is official policy never to reveal) and without really knowing how much space there might be to negotiate about conditions or medication. He had not seen the doctor's report which said medication was required, nor indeed most of the other statements about him which would influence official decisions. If we expect offenders to participate in decisions and to co-operate in efforts to resolve some of their own problems this suggests a second look at some of the characteristics and practices of our criminal justice system as a whole, and it is to some of these issues that we turn next.

7

State Coercion and Participatory Justice

The collapse of 'treatment' as a central rationale for penal policy creates problems not only for social work but for the wider criminal justice system. In recent years discussion of this problem has tended to polarise around the concepts of 'welfare' and 'justice' and the different implications of welfare and justice orientations for determining the goals of criminal justice practice. The last decade and a half have seen a series of well-argued critiques of 'welfare' models, ranging from attacks on the injustice involved in indeterminate sentencing of adults (e.g. American Friends' Service Committee 1971) to arguments that a more legalistic juvenile justice system is needed to protect children's rights (e.g. Morris, Giller, Szwed and Geach 1980). Principles of more determinate sentencing and less discretion for 'welfare' experts have received official endorsement in a number of American states and to some extent in Britain, for instance in the White Paper on young offenders (Home Office 1980) which preceded the 1982 Criminal Justice Act. Critics of 'welfare' models have come from all parts of the political spectrum, from radical sociologists on the left (e.g. Cohen 1979, Taylor, Lacey and Bracken 1980) to Conservative ideologues who have included such criticism in their general case against the Welfare State (Morgan 1978); however, what they have to say against 'welfare' models in criminal justice is remarkably consistent.

To equate delinquency with personal pathology or

deprivation is, they argue, a recipe for diminishing the personal responsibility of the offender and at the same time his rights, since handing his case over to the discretion of experts allows them to assume a high degree of coercive control without direct accountability, public access to decision-making or opportunities for clients to challenge decisions. In juvenile justice, the classic example of unfettered executive discretion has been the care order, which under the 1969 Children and Young Persons Act could leave juvenile offenders in the care of a local authority for an indeterminate period of up to eight years, with the local authority placing the child at will in his own home, in secure custodial accommodation or anywhere in between, often as the result of an offence for which an adult would have been unlikely to receive a custodial sentence at all. Critics point out that this kind of system reduces the rights of offenders to be protected against excessive intervention, and that it relies heavily on professional groups who may have their own interests to pursue; that it promises 'treatment' which is often ineffective; and that it can lead to more drastic intervention on 'treatment' grounds than would be justified purely by the seriousness of the offence. In the absence of substantial evidence to support claims that appropriate sentencing can either reform offenders or reduce crime by deterring others, critics of 'welfare' models return to classical ideas of just punishment or proportionate retribution based on an explicitly moral assessment of the seriousness of an offence. As Roger Hood puts it,

> I believe a system which arrives at the length of sentences based more on moral evaluation than on appeals to the utilitarian philosophy of deterrence and reductivism, would be fairer, not necessarily less effective, possibly less, not more, punitive and appeal to that sense of social justice on which any acceptable system of social control must be founded. (Hood 1974)

Thus the 'justice' model appears, at first sight, to be offering an attractive solution. It appears to fit neatly with other concerns in social policy about such matters as the rights of the mentally ill (Gostin 1977), the exclusion of natural parents from decision-making about children in care (One-Parent Families 1982) and the increasing demands of children in care for the right to be consulted about their future. It defines delinquency as a matter of opportunity and individual choice rather than pathology, holding offenders accountable in a common-sense way for their actions; proof of offence becomes the sole criterion for intervention, and like cases are to be treated alike, with the seriousness of the offence determining the level of response. 'Treatment' becomes separate from punishment, and presumably voluntary; the 'welfare experts' are put in their place, and the defendant (or his lawyer) becomes the focus of discussion about rights and duties. The complexities of individualised assessment can be happily abandoned in favour of a retributive tariff, and everyone's decisions become simpler, including those of the offender who simply has to weigh up the known penalties before deciding whether or not to risk an offence.

Such a model looks tidy on paper. It has proved particularly interesting to practitioners in the juvenile justice field, who have had to cope for more than a decade in England and Wales with a system based on an uneasy mixture of 'welfare' and 'justice' which seemed to produce little of either. I have already alluded in chapter 1 to the demoralizing effect of the 1969 Children and Young Persons Act, which aimed to reduce unnecessary prosecutions and to divert juveniles from custodial sentences and residential care, and seems on the whole to have had the opposite effect. But before we rush to embrace 'just deserts' as the answer to all our problems, it seems prudent to examine what is on offer a little more carefully.

WELFARE, JUSTICE AND PARTICIPATION

The 'just deserts' model is essentially an abstract attempt to construct a logical rationale for punishment in the absence of any consistent evidence that punishment is useful to offenders or to anyone else. In its attempt to accommodate our current empirical understanding of the results of penal practice, it becomes implicated in its own empirical implausibilities — for instance, the notion of the rational offender calmly weighing up profit and risk like a small businessman may fit some professional and white-collar crime, but hardly describes the impulsive thefts or expressive damage committed by groups of adolescents. Nor does it fit some of the most serious violent crimes which are often committed without thought of consequences, in moments of uncontrolled rage. But more fundamental problems emerge if we consider what it might be like to operate or participate in such a system. If sentences are to represent nothing but a carefully graduated quantity of coercive retribution, this may give us in principle a way of deciding on their length but it tells us very little about their *content*, which is a real practical problem for those involved in implementing penal programmes. What are we to do with the prisoner during his sentence, or the probationer during his order? The content of even very negative penal regimes, such as the old 'silent system' which segregated prisoners totally from each other, has always sought justification in terms of intended beneficial effects on the offender or society. A model which designs penal policy purely around a graduated tariff of retribution lends itself to no such justifications and provides no guidance as to the kind of demand to be made on offenders apart from simple deprivation of liberty. It relies on the infliction of controlled harm without any real expectation of benefit. Even the Victorian practice of filling the prisoner's idle hours with oakum-picking and the treadmill was supposed to do him good, but the 'just deserts' model includes no suggestions about doing anything at all once the length of sentence has been determined.

The model's claim to fairness also requires some critical examination. It is very difficult to make standardised penalties seem 'fair' in the light of common-sense moral assumptions when they are applied to offenders in very different circumstances. The able criminal with marketable skills, who could succeed without crime, seems in a different moral case from the deprived and unskilled person with few opportunities to avoid crime, even when they commit the same offence. By purporting to treat offenders equally in a society which has treated them unequally, the 'just deserts' model risks perpetuating and reinforcing the disadvantages of the poor by ignoring commonplace moral distinctions between those who have few legitimate opportunities and those who have many.

The goal of 'fairness' also appears more elusive if we consider how difficult it is to arrive at agreed judgements about the seriousness of offences. Most people would regard most violent offences as more serious than most property offences but beyond this we would expect considerable variation, even before we come to consider questions such as responsibility for unintended harm, or the opposite case of unsuccessful attempts at serious crime. Often only the detailed circumstances and backgrounds of particular incidents can throw light on issues of this kind, and so the quest for consistent justice pulls us back towards individualised consideration of individual cases. Some of the practical implications of this are explored further in the next chapter.

However, perhaps the most fundamental criticisms of justice model theorising concern its possible effects on the nature of proceedings and particularly on the participation of those most directly involved. Several criminologists, most notably Nils Christie (1982), have commented that the imposition of a standard set of fixed penalties depends heavily on the uniform exercise of centralised State power and removes the opportunity for discussion and participation in decisions not only from offenders, victims and local communities but potentially even from sentencers themselves. In a system of mandatory fixed sentencing their function could be reduced to the mechanical implementation of a predetermined list of sanctions. In this way the attempt to impose consistency through uniformity could result in outcomes which nobody could discuss or influence, and court hearings would be reduced to pure ceremonial with little or no decision-making function. Such criticisms are voiced even of current practices in criminal justice — defendants may feel excluded from proceedings by unfamiliarity and by the way the professionals take over the significant roles (Carlen 1976); and young offenders confess to researchers their realisation that police and courts are necessary, but constantly feel that their rights and interests are over-ridden by authorities who do not always keep their own rules. Howard Parker (1974) summarises their views: 'The necessity of Authority is thus not in question by either side. What is constantly in question is the behaviour of the officials who represent Authority.'

Even the victims of crime, whose interests are supposedly central to the system's operation, reveal in several studies (e.g. Shapland 1982, Maguire 1980) their sense of exclusion from the handling of 'their own' cases and their feeling that the system is not really interested in them except perhaps as potential witnesses if their offender is caught and (even more rarely) pleads not guilty. Nor are victims' expectations necessarily unrealistic or punitive: Maguire's burglary victims, for instance, often recognised and accepted that the offender might not be caught but still felt deprived of an 'appropriate' response to the loss and shock they had experienced. The British Crime Survey (Home Office 1983), the most comprehensive victim survey so far carried out in Britain, shows that most victims do not advocate severe sentences for 'their' offender, and many favour reparative or compensatory forms of sentence; nevertheless the widespread fear of crime and the growing realisation that victims are often the neglected parties in our criminal justice system point to aspects of the 'crime problem' to which our present criminal justice system makes no adequate response. The State has become a surrogate victim and harm done by offenders to victims is handled as if it is harm done by offenders to the State, which then exacts coercive penalties and treats the matter as settled. Justice models, in their search for consistency through imposed uniformity, risk increasing still further the coercive role of the State in criminal justice, at the expense of the potential participation of either victims or offenders.

David Matza takes a characteristically bleak view of the State's involvement in criminal justice, which is worth quoting at some length:

In its avid concern for public order and safety, implemented through police force and penal policy, Leviathan is vindicated. By pursuing evil and producing the *appearance* of good, the state reveals its abiding method — the perpetuation of its good name in the face of its own propensities for violence, conquest, and destruction. Guarded by a collective representation in which theft and violence reside in a dangerous class, morally elevated by its correctional quest, the state achieves the legitimacy of pacific intention and the appearance of legality — even if it goes to war and massively perpetrates activities it has allegedly banned from the world. (Matza 1969)

Certainly our criminal proceedings often seem far removed from the reality of the events they deal with, which sometimes seem to figure as little more than the raw material for a piece of symbolic theatre on a law and order theme. However, even if we take a more balanced view of the State as potentially beneficial as well as coercive, there are still serious questions to consider about participation and the balance of power in criminal justice decision-making.

Analysts of criminal justice policy, when considering the possibility of alternative systems, have tended in recent years to point in two directions. On the one hand some (like Hulsman 1983) invite us to consider the system of civil justice, in which harm done by one party to another is handled as a dispute between those parties and they are encouraged where possible to reach voluntary settlements. Avoidance of a formal hearing is seen as constructive and beneficial rather than as an evasion of justice, and it is not seen as particularly important if the outcomes of similar cases vary somewhat provided that the parties are satisfied. Formal adversarial proceedings are increasingly treated as a last resort. The recent history of law and practice in matrimonial proceedings illustrates this clearly: from a preoccupation with 'matrimonial offences' and the formal identification of the guilty party we have moved a long way towards a system in which the parties retain control of their dispute and are encouraged to find mutually tolerable solutions. The State, through its courts, increasingly performs the function of recognising and endorsing the parties' preferred solutions and ensuring that they are acceptable to the legal framework rather than imposing blame and sanctions. Even where the interests of vulnerable third parties such as children are involved, there is an increasing tendency to seek agreed solutions and where possible to facilitate these through conciliation procedures in which the parties are helped to negotiate effectively, with due recognition of their capacity to make decisions and their responsibility as parents. Social workers and probation officers with experience of these processes (e.g. Parkinson 1983) stress the need for a non-judgemental stance which encourages explicit dialogue between the parties rather than proxy negotiation through representatives. Clearly our civil jurisdiction offers a number of examples of a participatory approach to problem-solving which is often actively encouraged by State officials, and which is quite different from characteristic practice in criminal justice.

The other main direction in which critics point is towards systems of participatory justice in traditional societies and in societies which value high levels of popular participation in decisions. Christie (1977), for instance, argues that systems like ours deprive parties of their own conflicts, which he describes as an important form of 'property'. Direct participation by the parties can reinforce social bonds and allow disputes to be managed in a way that both reflects and clarifies community norms relating to the disputed behaviour. He gives examples of participatory systems in which all members of a village community have the opportunity to comment on and influence decisions, and suggests that such occasions provide important opportunities for the negotiation and restatement of values — precisely the kind of opportunity which is missing in the mechanical application of uniform 'justice models'. Anthropologists have also shown the variety and subtlety of systems of social control in so-called 'primitive' societies which maintain order without a centralised bureaucratic apparatus to impose it, and were originally regarded by early European visitors as lawless simply because they managed without a written criminal law (Roberts 1979).

Of course there can be no simple transplantation of systems and procedures from a peasant village or a gathering of tribal elders to a British criminal court, even if they are more satisfied with their systems than we are with ours. In a traditional society most 'crimes' will be between neighbours and all participants will know the background and circumstances well, in addition to a fund of information about the individual parties and their histories which goes far beyond what is available in a courtroom encounter with a labelled stranger. Equally, participation has its dangers: romantic left-idealist advocates of 'working-class justice' cannot explain away the absence of due process and natural justice in shop-floor kangaroo courts, or the extreme brutality and coerciveness of the 'justice' administered by some revolutionary movements (see, for instance, the study of informal paramilitary justice in Belfast by Morrissey and Pease 1982). We should also remember that there is a very high degree of community participation in a lynch-mob, and indeed that in our own history the anxiety of monarchs to establish a monopoly of criminal justice grew partly out of a concern to limit blood-feuds and private military adventures in pursuit of vengeance. People reasonably expect security from arbitrary interference as well as opportunities to influence decisions that affect them. A number of criminologists who were prominent in the sixties in arguing for a more appreciative and sympathetic stance towards the labelled deviant are now pointing out that the victims of crime are often poor, that exposure to high risks of crime constitutes a real social deprivation and that people's fears about crime and demands for effective crime control are understandable and to some extent justifiable (e.g. Taylor 1981). What is still in question is whether our criminal justice system can effectively meet these demands: that is, whether the harm it inflicts on offenders does anyone any good.

REMODELLING CRIMINAL JUSTICE

Despite these reservations about participatory justice, it is interesting that much recent official policy appears to accept some of the criticisms of a criminal justice system which seems to substitute for community involvement. In the last few years we have seen widespread new initiatives towards 'community policing' which were given an extra boost by the urban riots of 1981 and the Scarman Report (Home Office 1981b). These have their equivalents in other areas of State activity, where new policies for the care of the elderly and the handicapped stress 'community care', and a report on the role and tasks of local authority social workers argues imprecisely but at length for 'community social work' (Barclay 1982).

The uncritical acceptance of 'community' strategies has its dangers: often the notion of 'community' is employed simply as a slogan, and it has been described as an aerosol word which we spray over social problems in the hope that they will disappear. It can also be a disguise for cuts in public services by monetarist governments anxious to reduce tax burdens on the wealthy. However, it would be wrong to dismiss the recent vogue for community strategies as no more than sloganising. It points to some of the real deprivations experienced by the powerless consumers of bureaucratically organised services, and suggests strategies based on more involvement and wider participation. Even the Home Office, in a recent document on objectives and priorities in the probation service, endorses the notion of more community involvement and stresses that crime is a problem for the whole community which calls for a broadly based response (Home Office 1984). It also gives several examples of possible strategies for community involvement by probation services, and although its proposals are somewhat ambiguous it shows that the problems of public participation in resolving criminal justice problems have not escaped official awareness. It is not enough, however, to make vague appeals to 'community' and 'participation'. These may conjure up images of village elders benevolently resolving disputes under a tree, but they also conjure up the menacing figures of the vigilante and the lynch-mob. While wide community co-operation may be essential in crime-prevention strategies, participation in dispute-management must be by the parties most directly involved; the kangaroo court is wrong not because it lacks community participation but because it fails to respect offenders' rights and imposes outcomes in a coercive way by force of numbers. Coercion and participation are, as we have seen, closely related issues; processes which respect persons also respect the capacity for choice, and a shift in emphasis from 'treatment' to 'help' is a shift away from coercion by experts towards participation by clients. Our criminal justice system is characterised not only by low levels of real participation but by high levels of coercion, for instance in its overuse of custodial sentences and its preoccupation with doing things to offenders rather than with what offenders can do for the community or for themselves.

Custodial coercion is a scarce resource, expensive and ultimately damaging, but the drift towards increased coercion seems difficult to control despite official concern. Any attempt to identify the deficiencies of our criminal justice system must consider not only participation but the linked issue of overreliance on coercion. The last few chapters have presented a case for a participatory and problem-solving model of social work, in which negotiated and agreed outcomes are preferred to imposed goals and one-sided procedures. Any attempt to increase the role of participatory problem-solving in criminal justice will require a similar weakening of coercive assumptions, whether of a 'welfare model' ('We know what's good for you') kind or of a more overtly punitive 'just deserts' variety.

It will also require a slight change in our common-sense assumptions about justice. For example, it has been pointed out that mediation schemes in which victim and offender meet with a third party to discuss possible ways of 'making good' the offence, as an alternative to a solution imposed by the court, may have inconsistent outcomes, since what is regarded as sufficient atonement will depend not only on what the offender has done but on how the victim reacts, how they perceive each other when they meet, and so on. Thus similar cases may have dissimilar results, and critics can argue that this offends against the principle of treating like cases alike. Existing sentencing practice may show far less consistency than it theoretically should; however, it is clear that a greater reliance on participatory arrangements such as mediation schemes would also lead to substantial variety in outcomes. Our criteria of 'justice' perhaps need to pay less attention to uniformity, which in our system is usually an imposed uniformity, and more attention to whether outcomes are acceptable to the parties most directly involved. What they perceive as fair and reasonable may vary, but this could be better than an imposed system of 'just deserts' which is not perceived as fair. Participatory decision-making is likely to result in individualised outcomes, but these individual differences would derive directly from the perceptions and interests of the parties rather than from some expert's one-sided diagnosis.

Our existing system, despite its rhetoric of justice and order, seems to be involved in a vicious circle. By frustrating victims and failing to achieve its stated policy objectives it increases community anxiety about crime; this leads in turn to demands for more effective measures, to which we respond with more custodial punishment. This reduces opportunities for offenders to resolve problems constructively or to make any more direct kind of reparation; consequently victim frustration increases, and so on. It also reduces opportunities for the community to encounter offenders in any positive or personal way, such as through involvement in community programmes or in reparation. The offender then remains an anonymous threat or a mass media stereotype, and the British Crime Survey reminds us that for many people the fear of crime and criminals is a greater problem than the actual risk of crime. Attempts to improve the provision of criminal justice and to break into this kind of vicious circle will need to embody the two linked aims of reducing reliance on coercive strategies and of increasing active participation by offenders, victims and the community, both in decision-making and in the implementation of decisions. Such a strategy could preserve and enhance the advantages of individualised decision-making, while also reflecting the justice model's arguments that criminal justice decisions are moral decisions based on values rather than on techniques of treatment.

In case this seems an unrealistically Utopian programme, it is interesting to consider how far some of these concerns are already reflected in some areas of criminal justice practice. For instance, victims are routinely consulted when the police decide whether to caution or prosecute juveniles, and in one experimental scheme the participation of victims is linked to the possibility of reparation (Blagg and Derricourt forthcoming). Victim support schemes, in which volunteers visit and try to help victims of crime, have grown from one scheme in 1974 to about 190 at the time of writing, becoming the fastest growing voluntary organisation in the criminal justice field and showing not only the extent of public concern but also the extent to which people are prepared to participate constructively in doing something about a problem (NAVSS 1984). A number of reparation schemes are being planned or are beginning to function following enthusiastic advocacy by criminal justice professionals who have looked at their operation in other countries (e.g. Harding 1982; Wright 1982).

Even within the routine everyday practices of the criminal justice system there are striking differences in the extent to which different sentences invite or require active participation by offenders. Conventional distinctions between 'welfare-model' sentencing and 'justice-model' sentencing (or between high and low individualisation in criminal justice decisions) may tend to blur the issue of participation: for instance, mandatory prison terms are a low-individualisation measure and compulsory psychiatric treatment highly individualised, but both are highly coercive, as is the indeterminate juvenile care order which is often seen as the classic welfare-model sentence. Probation, on the other hand, potentially allows a high degree of offender participation; community service, although a more determinate sentence than probation (since the total hours of community service are fixed at the time of sentence, unlike the amount of contact between officer and probationer), also offers substantial scope for participation by offenders, beneficiaries and volunteers. The popularity of community service may have something to do with the opportunities it offers for constructive participation.

The existing system also offers space for participation which is currently underused, such as the opportunity for social workers, probation officers and offenders to influence sentencing decisions through the social inquiry process. This process has often been seen in 'treatment model' terms, with the social inquiry report representing an expert diagnosis of the offender and incorporating advice about the appropriate treatment, and as such it has been heavily criticised by advocates of justice models (e.g. Bean 1976). But it also represents an important opportunity to influence sentencing in the direction of objectives other than 'treatment'. Although some critics of the 1969 Children and Young Persons Act have written as if it failed for the curiously abstract reason that it embodied philosophical ambiguities between 'welfare' and 'justice' models, others have argued from a more practical point of view that whatever its defects, it did include substantial opportunities for diversion away from custody. These, however, were not often used because social workers did not recommend them often enough in social inquiry reports (Thorpe, Smith, Green and Paley 1980). Conversely, of course, the opportunities could have been used; in other words, the microsystem of criminal justice decision-making has some relative autonomy and some flexibility which can be exploited to improve the quality of its results.

The recent 1982 Criminal Justice Act reflects in some ways the 'law and order' preoccupations of a Conservative Government and gives the courts a wider range of custodial options for young offenders. It also reflects some of the concerns of the 'justice model' lobby by replacing indeterminate Borstal sentences with determinate Youth Custody and restricting local authorities' rights to keep children in secure accommodation without a court's permission. However, it also introduces an enlarged range of potentially diversionary provisions and limits the powers of courts to impose custodial sentences except in those cases where offences are judged to be relatively serious or offenders are unable or unwilling to comply with non-custodial sentences. Social workers and probation officers are in a good position to influence these key factors of feasibility and willingness, and to offer appropriate diversionary alternatives in their social inquiry reports.

The Act itself, supported by recent Home Office circulars (e.g. HOC 18/1983), encourages an energetic approach to the development of local non-custodial projects as adjuncts to supervision and probation orders. Sadly, the new custodial sentences, efficiently provided by central government, have been available (and used) since May 1983, while the local authorities and voluntary bodies have been slower to produce the non-custodial alternatives; the probation service has done a little better, but there are worrying signs that the experience of the 1969 Act may be about to repeat itself. For instance, a recent survey of social inquiry reports on young offenders entering a detention centre finds no sign that report writers are yet addressing the specific requirements of the 1982 Act in their reports (Nottinghamshire Probation Service 1984).

If we accept, as I think we must, the 'just deserts' argument that the extent of the demands made by a court on an offender as a consequence of his offence should reflect a moral evaluation of the offence and its circumstances rather than any spurious 'treatment' logic, there is still a large and crucial area of flexibility in determining how those demands should be met. It is here that the social inquiry report can exercise an important influence as a negotiating document and an instrument of participation. Whatever the defects of the existing system, the social inquiry process represents a current opportunity for progress in the direction of a more problem-solving and less coercive practice. The next chapter explores some of the issues involved in this admittedly reformist and non-Utopian, and therefore feasible, strategy.

8

Social Inquiry as
Court-Based Negotiation

The arguments of the previous chapter suggest that if
social work with offenders is to play an effective part in
improving the operation of the criminal justice system,
this might be done by encouraging the development of
less coercive and more participatory methods of managing
some of the disputes which provide the 'raw material' of
criminal justice. We should no longer simply ask ourselves
'Are we providing effective treatments?' or 'Are we
inflicting consistent punishment?', but should consider
whether we are providing opportunities for those involved
in and affected by offences to be dealt with in ways that
respect their perceptions, responsibilities, needs and
potential contribution to setting matters right. The
institution of criminal justice then appears not as a set of
arrangements for eliminating crime (which it cannot do)
but as a system whose outcomes can contribute to a more
satisfactory way of living with the consequences of crime.
Possibilities of this kind seem to lie in the pursuit of the
two linked aims of promoting constructive participation
and reducing avoidable coercion. Social work in many
fields has been moving towards a more participatory and
humanistic model in which the ideas of diagnosis and
treatment give way to procedures based on negotiation
and agreed help; the increasing acceptance and adoption
of methods such as task-centred casework (Reid and
Epstein 1972) provide one example of this. Similarly, it is

suggested that a common theme in several recent criticisms of criminal justice systems is the advocacy of a significant shift from coercive to contractual approaches, and towards the greater involvement of the parties in decisions about what is, after all, their affair. The question 'Why should the criminal justice system be interested in helping offenders?' becomes more accessible once we recognise that crude retribution is not the only alternative to ineffective 'treatment'.

However, any attempt to develop a 'non-treatment' model of the social worker's role in criminal justice is faced with the problem of providing a rationale for social work's most frequent contribution to the courts' decisions, namely the practice of providing social inquiry reports on individual offenders. In the age of 'rehabilitation through casework' such a rationale was easy to find: the reports could be seen, at least by their providers, as diagnostic documents recommending the most effective treatment. But if we now find this model hard to defend, why is it that the courts' demand for such a service shows no sign of fading away? On the contrary, new laws regularly increase the range of situations in which sentencers are obliged to consider the kind of information reports contain, and the demand for reports remained buoyant even during years when the demand for other social work products such as probation orders and supervision orders fell. In many areas probation officers spend a large proportion of their time on reports. Courts clearly expect them, usually want them and sometimes seem almost dependent on them. But what purpose do they serve?

SOCIAL INFORMATION AND JUSTICE

There is no need to review at length here the many reasons which have been given for questioning the effectiveness of the social inquiry report as a 'treatment' document. The arguments are similar to those deployed against the 'treatment' model in general: for example, we find that the regular use of social inquiries does not significantly reduce recidivism (Hood 1966), and that they are inconsistent in length and coverage, sometimes containing unverified information of doubtful status (Perry 1974). Although high levels of agreement between reports' recommendations and eventual sentences are regularly reported (for instance by Thorpe and Pease 1976), such studies leave us uncertain as to whether the reports have influenced the sentencers or whether the report writers have tailored their documents to fit anticipated outcomes. Some studies (such as Hine, McWilliams and Pease 1978) suggest that there can be an influence in some cases, but this influence can hardly be in any consistent direction when other research shows that report writers shift unpredictably between different frames of reference and different approaches to the report's function. This appears clearly, for instance, in Hardiker's demonstration (1977) of contradictory ideologies of treatment within a sample of reports. Sometimes the researchers who point to incomplete information also criticise reports for containing far more information than is really needed for sentencing (for example Bean 1976); the same writer has suggested that recommendations depend more on the characteristics of the officer than on those of the offender, and that reports tend to mask moral and evaluative judgements in purportedly 'neutral' and 'objective' diagnostic statements.

Such arguments will be familiar from previous chapters and effectively undermine claims that social inquiries function as a scientific aid to 'treatment'; often the suggested remedy will be some version of our old friend the 'justice model', sometimes coupled with a suggestion that reports can be eliminated altogether or reduced to a few straightforward, easily verifiable and perhaps not very interesting 'facts'. Indeed anyone who examines a sample of social inquiry reports, whether for professional or research purposes, will often be struck by apparent omissions, inconsistencies, jargon, unclear reasoning and occasionally prejudicial statements. Similar criticisms can be made of other reports presented to sentencers, and such reports represent bad practice whatever function they were intended to serve; they should perhaps be taken as evidence of uneven performance, and possibly of uncertainty about what a good performance would be, rather than as evidence that there is no useful task involved or that attempts to perform it are unnecessary. It is not very useful to condemn bad practice unless one has some notion of what good practice would be, and it is here that critics of the social inquiry process find themselves in difficulty, with different writers citing the same deficiencies as evidence of the need for more thorough reports or of the need for no reports at all. Those who still believe in the possibility of scientific sentencing will advocate more scientific reports; those who prefer a model of strict tariff sentencing with little consideration of individual differences will prefer simplified reports or no reports; and practitioners will find that research offers little consistent guidance about the direction in which improvement should occur. However, a consideration of possible rationales for 'non-treatment' sentencing can throw some light on the function of social information in criminal justice decisions.

It is not true, for instance, that the use of social information in sentencing necessarily implies a commitment to 'diagnosis and treatment'. Studies of sentencing practice and of reasons given for particular sentences (e.g. Thomas 1964) show a complicated interaction between 'tariff' considerations and individualised concerns. Sentencers do seem to have in mind a retributive tariff of graded severity related to the perceived seriousness of offences, and they also employ a range of individualised sentences which are deliberate and conscious departures from the tariff. Although we have become used to thinking of individualised sentences as 'welfare model' treatment decisions, sentencing an offender for his background rather than his offence, there is also a strong tradition of individualised justice which is much older and more deeply rooted than any ideas about the scientific treatment of criminals. This tradition has its roots partly in the ideas of participatory and negotiated justice explored in the last chapter: that is, in the search for outcomes which reflect the particular circumstances and significance of events as perceived by participants. It also has a firm base in some of our everyday moral assumptions about justice.

The moral basis of many of our ideas about individual-ised sentencing is best illustrated by considering the rather different meanings and usages of the legal notion of 'guilt' and the moral notion of 'blameworthiness'. Legal guilt is a very black-and-white affair — I am guilty if the law forbids what I did, and if I was not insane or compelled by some other person when I did it. Whether I am blameworthy, in the moral sense, is much more a matter of degree, and involves many more shades of grey. It may depend, for instance, on what I intended to do; on whether I was adequately informed about the circumstances in which I acted; on whether I was capable of alternative courses of action; on whether I was under unusual stress; on whether I was confused; or on whether I was brought up in such a way as not to regard my action as wrong. Many possible circumstances could allow my action to be seen as less than wholly blameworthy, or less than deliberately criminal. Often there is a fair amount of agreement among ordinary people, and between ordinary people and sentencers, that these are the sort of considerations that should determine how much blame we attribute to an offender for his offence. There is, of course, considerable scope for variations in the relative moral weight we attach to considerations of this kind, and sentencers could certainly be more specific about the moral reasoning behind their sentences; nevertheless, they do illustrate how punishments for the same offence could vary in ways that most people would recognise as just. They also illustrate that arriving at some estimate of blameworthiness is not a purely arbitrary business, but depends partly on factual questions, since each of the considerations listed above refers to a state of affairs about which factual information could, in principle, be available. In court proceedings it often seems that social information is used very much in this way, as a basis for considering how far the offender can be blamed and punished or alternatively seen as deserving leniency. Even when the 'treatment' model takes over and evidence of social or personal problems becomes a reason for *more* coercive intervention, this will tend to be presented as more help rather than as more punishment.

As well as resting on common-sense moral foundations, individualised justice has a long history. We have seen in the last chapter how societies without a centralised State, a formal criminal justice system or law-enforcement officials must have other ways of righting wrongs. Disputes between neighbours must be settled between neighbours or by some form of local community mediation. The norm is likely to be some kind of reparation, either offered or exacted. It may be material (like handing back stolen property) or symbolic (like paying money to a murdered man's kin or being killed by them). The origins of our ideas of retribution (i.e. of visiting harm on the offender which corresponds to the harm he has done) may lie in this kind of primitive reparation. Our system of civil law still works on the principle of reparation, but many of the actions now defined as criminal would once have been dealt with in the same way. The idea that a wrong done to your fellow citizen is also a wrong done to the State (or the Crown, or the King's Peace) is a later development, attributable in this country largely to the attempts of Anglo-Saxon kings to impose an orderly and centralised system of State justice to moderate the inconvenience and variety of traditional dispute procedures (Sylvester 1977). We now have a complex system of State justice, in which the criminal law forbids a wide range of actions, State officials prosecute and sentence on behalf of the Crown, and the victim does not usually benefit directly. The hallmark of criminal justice mediated by the centralised State is retribution rather than reparation, imposing penalties by the exercise of power rather than developing compromise solutions through a process of conflict management.

Even now, the official criminal justice system deals only with the tip of the iceberg of crime, and many offences are still dealt with unofficially. Elements of the unofficial system have been incorporated here and there as diversionary opportunities in the State system, designed to 'filter out' certain categories of offender from further coercive processing as in the practice of formal police cautions instead of prosecution for some juveniles. There are also strong possibilities that Britain will follow other countries in including elements of victim—offender mediation and reparation in the official system. Without digressing at this stage into a detailed discussion of these prospects, it seems that the tradition of individualised justice has a respectable history long before the 'Age of Rehabilitation', and is still very much alive as a source of alternatives to retribution.

Another important feature of this kind of individualised justice is that it tends to be *contractual.* It is often based on the premise that the offender can be restored to his normal status as a participating member of the community provided that he gives certain undertakings about what he will do to right the wrong, and abides by those undertakings. In other words, individualised justice is not simply a watered-down version of tariff justice; it can involve a different kind of outcome altogether, in which an agreement is reached between the offender and those he has offended, or between the offender and the official system.

In contemporary sentencing, we see in some cases a reduction of the tariff sentence because something in the offender or his circumstances suggests that he is less blameworthy than the 'norm' for that kind of offence. The light sentences recently given to battered wives who have killed their husbands are an example of this. In other cases we see the court deciding not to exercise its right to punish, or to exercise it to a limited extent only, as a result of some agreement reached with the offender in which both parties are prepared to compromise. (They are not, of course, equal parties, but agreements between unequal parties need not be imposed agreements.) Conditional discharge, deferred sentence, community service and probation all have, at least in a formal sense, this kind of contractual structure.

These arguments about individualised justice and the moral basis of sentencing suggest that the provision of social information about offenders can have at least two important functions, neither of which presupposes a 'treatment' model. One function is in relation to the assessment of blameworthiness or moral culpability; the other is in relation to the scope for individualised sentencing, and particularly for contractual sentencing.

SENTENCING AS PROBLEM-SOLVING

The main relevance of social information to questions of moral culpability lies in helping the sentencer to assess blameworthiness, perhaps along a continuum from 'he almost couldn't help acting as he did' to 'he acted in full knowledge of what he was doing, with calculated indifference to the harm done to others, after long and careful planning to maximise gain and minimise risk to himself.' Information about circumstances and background helps to throw light on how far the offender could reasonably have been expected to act differently, and how far he can be held morally responsible for not doing so. Our criminal justice system, and most of us for all practical purposes, assume a degree of free will and choice about some actions, without which any notions of guilt, blame and desert become meaningless. We believe we can to some extent choose what we do, but some choices are harder than others, and all choices are subject to constraints and influence. Social inquiry reports can help to illuminate these constraints and influences as they affect the choices and actions of a particular individual.

The social sciences offer many possible frameworks for understanding and illuminating the social influences on individual action, and this is not the place to engage in lengthy discussion of the merits and deficiencies of competing frameworks. However, it is clear that any explanatory framework which is likely to be useful in a context of concern about justice must be one which recognises a degree of relative autonomy in individual choice and can allow us to distinguish situations in which people have very few options from those in which they have many. This will tend to rule out crude varieties of both sociological and psychological determinism: as passive puppets, whether of social circumstances or of inner drives, we can hardly be held responsible for anything. One example (there are many others) of a position between these extremes can be found in some of the work of the Centre for Contemporary Cultural Studies, which invites us to consider the respective contributions of *structure, culture,* and *biography* (Critcher 1976). In this framework, the constraints of structure are those basic economic and material factors which set the limits of an individual's opportunities, and the constraints of culture are the strengths and weaknesses of the way he has learned, along with other members of his social group, to assimilate, make sense of and operate within the limits of structure. Biography refers to the multitude of contingencies or accidents of experience that distinguish one individual from another, even within the same cultural and structural space. For instance, one person can run faster than another, and may consequently get away with more. If we add personality, or individual tendencies to show particular kinds of behaviour, to this list of levels of explanation, we have quite a useful summary of the kinds of information which can be included in a report and which help to 'situate' and make sense of an individual's behaviour in the context of his life in society.

Information about the offence itself is also highly relevant in judgements of seriousness. It is only by understanding, as far as possible, the offender's own view of the offence and its circumstances that we can begin to think about what he intended, and how far he had a clear understanding of what was going on. The basic facts of the offence as presented through police evidence are often deficient in this kind of information. The task of acquiring it needs to be approached with what Matza (1969) calls 'appreciation', that is, the attempt to understand the offender's perspective 'from the inside'. This kind of exploration may be more easily carried out by social workers with some training and experience in helping people to express their views and feelings than by other court personnel whose preoccupations are often different.

One objection to this line of argument could be that I seem to be suggesting that social workers should concern themselves closely with moral evaluations and even with issues like blameworthiness, when the traditions of the profession would stress other values such as 'non-judgementalism'. However, we have seen that one reason for questioning the 'treatment model' is based on respect for persons as moral agents, capable of choice and responsibility. Any coherent interpretation of 'non-judgemental-ism' must therefore refer to a commitment to the value of persons despite their behaviour rather than to a refusal to be involved in any assessment of that behaviour. If processes of negotiation and dialogue in social work are partly about what people *ought* to do, they necessarily involve questions of moral evaluation. Nor am I advocating that probation officers themselves take on the task of moral evaluation in sentencing — simply that they recognise that this is an important use of the information they provide in the sentencing process, even if it is disguised as value-free 'diagnosis'. The report does not determine the moral evaluation, but contains some of the facts on which the sentencer can base his own moral reasoning. It is the court's job, not the social worker's, to judge issues such as seriousness.

Even so, the role I have outlined is bound to be uncomfortable for probation officers or social workers who have little sympathy with some of the moral assumptions of the criminal law, not least because it will involve contributing to a very unfavourable moral evaluation of some offences. Nevertheless, there may be some advantages in this discomfort. If we accept the necessity for systems of social control which are concerned about moral issues like seriousness and harm, we will still find plenty to criticise in the existing system; the point is not to 'fit in' with it, as I suspect probation officers and social workers often do, but to approach it as a target for change and improvement. Discomfort can then be constructive instead of simply a focus for helpless grumbling. In any case, a more rational approach to moral issues in sentencing seems more likely to benefit offenders than to increase the harm done to them, since it will tend to reduce the risk of more coercive intervention on 'treatment' grounds or on the basis of unreliable predictions about future behaviour. It also opens up the possibility of a more productive interaction between criminal justice and social justice. Any realistic evaluation of the background of many offenders will make it clear that they are also victims, and some people have few alternatives to crime in a society which distributes resources and power so unevenly. A more careful consideration of moral questions in sentencing could allow such issues to be raised more often.

Social information, then, can make an important contribution to a fair and morally reasonable system of sentencing. Such information about the offender and the offence will be mainly backward-looking and concerned with past events. The second major function of social inquiry reports lies in the exploration of sentencing options and particularly of the potential for a contractual approach to sentencing. Here the information will be more forward-looking and more the product of negotiation. In such a model, the emphasis would be not so much on 'prognosis' or purportedly scientific prediction as on a systematic examination, jointly with the offender, of such questions as what difficulties he has; how far he is prepared to recognise a need to change his way of dealing with problems in order to avoid trouble with the law; what undertakings he is prepared to give, and how realistic they are; and whether there is any help that might be provided. This requires a good deal of attention, care and skill in obtaining information for reports, and re-emphasises the social work content of the job. All probation officers know that good social inquiry interviewing is very different from getting facts to fill in a form.

On this model, any opinion expressed in the report about the appropriateness of some form of contractual sentencing should arise out of negotiation between the officer and defendant, and should carry the defendant's consent. It should be *offered* to the court as a plausible alternative to the retributive tariff sentence, not *recommended* as an expertly selected treatment based on a scientific diagnosis. The important issues are what the offender is prepared to do, whether and how far the social work agency is able to help him do it, and what assurances the court will require from both parties. What little evidence we have suggests that supervision is most likely to be helpful to offenders when it arises from their choice to make use of it, and when there is some degree of 'fit' between the kind of help offered and the difficulties the offender is aware of in his own life. I suspect that more attention to the role of social inquiry in exploring the basis for future help would lead to better and more purposeful supervision, and possibly to more probation orders being suggested and made. Nor should contractual work necessarily be confined to situations of formal supervision. For instance, the deferred sentence, with its expectation of concrete improvements within a specified time-scale, seems almost tailor-made for the practice of task-centred casework, and may be a realistic and useful context within which to offer voluntary supervision on a contractual basis.

To emphasise these aspects of social inquiry work may require some changes in attitude. Instead of concentrating the attention purely on the offender and his characteristics and 'needs', the suggested focus is a dual concern with the offender *and* his place in the criminal justice system. Reports become attempts to intervene in that system to produce change, and the direction of change needs to reflect policy choices about what kind of system is desirable. But the social work input into criminal justice is often far from dominant, and is only one source of influence among many others. Social workers and probation officers can influence the system but not compel it. The conclusions of reports offer a possible solution, or range of solutions, to courts and offenders, but they should not pretend to be the only influence on outcome. When sentencers criticise social inquiry reports for 'unrealistic recommendations' on the grounds that the offender deserves more punishment, they fall into the trap of believing that the function of a report is to recommend the appropriate sentence, and many providers of reports no doubt see it the same way; this puts the officer in a difficult position, requiring him to weigh up all factors in sentencing when only the court itself has the legitimate power to do this. A more realistic and less confusing approach would be to see courts as empowered to weigh issues of seriousness and the extent to which an offender's liberty should be restricted, while the reporting officer outlines possible courses of action which the court might wish to choose, with information about their feasibility and the likelihood of compliance. Whether the offender 'deserves' more is a matter for the court, not for the officer to guess at in an attempt to be 'realistic'. It has been suggested that such distinctions would be clearer if reports were divided into two parts, one of which concentrated on background and circumstances and the other on the available sentencing options and their likely effects.

CONTRACTS AND DIVERSION

This clear distinction between the sentencing function of courts and the enabling function of social inquiry reports also underlines an important feature of much contractual sentencing — namely that the contracts involved are between three parties: the court, the defendant and the supervising agency. The court is reserving or suspending part of its power to punish on the basis of an agreement with an offender who accepts a degree of responsibility for the offence, for complying with the court's demands, and in some cases for taking action to 'make good' the offence — for instance through symbolic reparation, as in a community service order, or through an attempt to resolve problems associated with the circumstances in which the offence occurred, as in many probation orders. If these undertakings are broken without good reason the basis for the court's decision disappears and the decision can be reviewed and changed. The court is also responsible for ensuring that the level of demand made on offenders, in terms of restrictions on their liberty, is a just outcome in relation to the perceived seriousness of the offence in its real context.

The supervising agency can be seen as responsible to the court for monitoring the offender's compliance with these agreements and reporting any serious breach and its circumstances, not necessarily with a view to punishment but perhaps with a suggestion of different and more feasible agreements. The agency's contract with the client involves respect, negotiation, facilitating compliance with agreements and, if agreed as a 'subsidiary contract' (Bryant et al. 1978), the provision of appropriate help. If there is no 'subsidiary contract' the client's responsibility to the agency is limited to the demands made by the court, and in any case no breach action can arise from a subsidiary contract which is in essence a voluntary agreement between client and agency going beyond the specific demands of the court. Another way to describe this is that the authority to make demands on offenders stems from, and is limited by, the court; the authority to help comes from the client. In this way elements of choice and participation can be clarified and preserved even within a system of real constraint.

Some writers (such as Wright 1982) have suggested that courts could limit themselves to specifying an appropriate level of demand, for instance on a points system, leaving it to offenders and supervising agencies to propose ways of making up the appropriate points score through various non-custodial or even custodial packages. Such a system would lay down clear equivalencies between, say, so many days in custody and so many hours of community service or months of probation. This would clarify choices for all parties, but seems a long way from current realities. A more achievable reform would be if courts, in requesting reports, were to indicate more clearly what range of penalties they have in mind, so that offenders faced with the possibility of entering into agreements around a probation order or community service order would have a clear idea whether the alternative is two years in prison or a £50 fine. Such considerations enter into decisions already, but tend to be based on guesses drawn from probation officers' or offenders' experience of the system and may be unreliable — for instance, there is some evidence that probation officers tend to overpredict the likelihood of custodial sentences (Crow, Pease and Hillary 1980). They may therefore offer alternatives at too high a tariff level, with all the attendant risks of accelerating their clients' progress into custody by attempting to make their recommendations 'realistic'.

A more realistic and feasible policy for current circumstances would be to concentrate on opportunities for diversion towards less coercive options, and to negotiate with offenders about how they might be able to meet demands somewhere near the level that the court is likely to set. For instance, there seems little justification for presenting custodial options to the court, since these would not normally be beneficial or constructive for the offender and should only be imposed where considerations of seriousness or public safety require them. These are considerations for the sentencer rather than the officer, and much recommending of custodial sentences could be eliminated by a systematic search for and development of less coercive alternatives. (This applies also to the covert recommendation of custody on treatment grounds: arguments like 'a period in a detention centre would help him to complete his education' cannot stand up to much scrutiny, and 'this young man would benefit from a structured environment' is simply a custodial recommendation in code.) Where there is clearly no possible non-custodial resource available, reports could simply state this fact, which is sometimes more a comment on local services than on the potential of the offender. ·

The implications of such a strategy in practice can be illustrated by considering the 'tariff' now available for the older range of juvenile offenders under the 1982 Criminal Justice Act. This includes more 'steps' than ever before, which can be outlined as follows:

non-custodial: conditional discharge
fine
attendance centre
supervision order
supervision order with discretionary
   intermediate treatment requirements
supervision order with non-
   discretionary supervised activity
   requirements
supervision order with 'negative'
   requirements
community service (if aged 16)

semi-custodial: care order

custodial: residential care order
detention centre
youth custody

Three of the non-custodial options are additions to the tariff of the 1969 Children and Young Persons Act, but the inclusion of new steps does not by itself guarantee that offenders will take longer to reach the top; 'what is constantly in question is the behaviour of the officials who represent Authority', and the effects of the new system will depend on how the courts are encouraged to use it. We have already encountered evidence that some children were propelled very fast up the old tariff by overcoercive intervention at too early a stage in their offending careers, often motivated by 'welfare' considerations. The arguments of the last two chapters suggest a feasible alternative policy in the use of social inquiry reports, namely to ensure that offenders move slowly rather than quickly through the tariff, so that most of them would 'grow out' of offending before reaching the top. For offenders in or near the lower end, this would mean offering, and arguing for, the least coercive feasible intervention. For offenders with records serious enough to place them in the higher (or, as it has become known, 'heavy') end, the appropriate policy would be to offer credible non-custodial alternatives which could contain them within or return them to the non-custodial band. This would also mean that agencies and supervisors would need to ensure that such alternatives were available, and some of the problems this raises are explored in a later chapter; however, unless such developments occur and are linked to the systematic pursuit of appropriate policies in social inquiry work, we can probably expect the 1982 Act to repeat the history of the 1969 Act. (Similar considerations apply to adult offenders, where the introduction of new variants of the traditional probation order potentially extends the range of non-custodial options in a very similar way.)

Agencies adopting such a strategy would normally need to begin with a systematic review of the operation of their local criminal justice system to establish the scope and target groups of diversion, by finding out what kinds of offenders are being sentenced to custody and what contribution social workers and probation officers are making to the current state of affairs. Several such studies have been undertaken (see, for instance, Thorpe, Smith, Green and Paley 1980) and have resulted in the adoption of systematic diversion strategies, as well as reductions in unnecessary residential care placements and the development of new non-custodial provisions. In one area (reported by Johnson, O'Hanlon and Mulcahy 1984) social workers have even encouraged a policy of appeals to higher courts against custodial sentences imposed by lower courts, with considerable success. However, one can also point to many areas in which avoidable custodial sentences are the routine experience of many young people in trouble and social agencies react as if this is inevitable or even desirable (after all, a young offender in an intensive intermediate treatment scheme is costing the local authority money, whereas the far heavier bill for his board and lodging in youth custody is paid by central government). We know a good deal now about how to achieve the desired effects on the criminal justice system, but implementation is a matter of political will or agency policy and remains patchy. Nevertheless, the strategy proposed is not particularly new or radical; diversion was the central intention of Parliament when the 1969 Children and Young Persons Act was passed, and there is nothing in the ideas outlined in this chapter which would be inconsistent with recent Government advice on social inquiries as contained in Home Office Circulars 17/1983 and 18/1983. The recent Home Office statement of 'national objectives and priorities' for the probation service identifies diversion from custody as a very high priority (Home Office 1984), and this must imply a systematically diversionary strategy in social inquiry reports.

ENLARGING THE NEGOTIATING SYSTEM

Attempts to influence local criminal justice policy may have their most obvious and direct expression in court, and the active presence of probation officers and social workers there seems crucial to their success, even if this presence runs counter to a recent trend of withdrawing from the courtroom into an office-based 'professionalism' (McWilliams 1981). However, attempts to involve sentencers and discuss alternative possibilities with them need not stop in the courtroom but can spread to probation liaison committees, crime prevention panels, local community bodies and even the design and management of diversionary projects. Community service may owe some of its popularity to the energetic attempts made to 'sell' it to sentencers and the enthusiastic identification of many magistrates with the early schemes; other diversionary projects have involved sentencers as active members of management committees, influencing both the project and their colleagues, and providing a further dimension to the three-party negotiating system within which contractual sentencing necessarily operates.

The possibility, and current use in many areas, of this strategy of negotiation and influence suggests that the aims of reducing coercion and increasing participation in criminal justice decision-making are not unrealistic; rather they are implicit in and prefigured by many features of current practice. There are also hints of a wider negotiating system, in which victims and local communities could play a fuller part and agreements could begin to involve five parties (court, offender, agency, victim and 'community') rather than three. However, it would be pointless to pretend that there are not other more disturbing possibilities implicit in the ascendancy of 'law and order' politicians, the widening of police powers, the erosion of civil liberties and the costly new prison building programme. The attempt to enlarge the role of non-coercive problem-solving will be made at a time when there is a very real prospect of a more authoritarian and more coercive society. This is partly why such an attempt seems necessary, and I have argued that it is feasible, but success is by no means guaranteed. Inaction will, however, guarantee failure. A number of different futures are possible for social work with offenders, and the final part of this book sets out to explore some of the more practical possibilities.

PART III

Feasible Change

Thus, after several hundred years of wandering in the wilderness of philosophy, the country reached the conclusions that commonsense had long since arrived at.

Samuel Butler, 'Erewhon', chapter XXVII

9

Futuristic Probation

Prediction in social matters is a hazardous business, and often wrong. Persuasive fictions can be disguised as fact, and the optimism or pessimism of the predictor's temperament moulds the uncontrolled variables to suit the preferred picture. It seems more honest, when indulging in almost pure speculation, to adopt an explicitly fictional form. The reader is therefore invited to project himself or herself 15 or 20 years into the future, discounting for the time being the possibility of global disaster, and to consider what kind of social work services we might by then be providing in and around the criminal justice system. As we have so far been concerned with identifying the conflicting present tendencies which will structure our future options, it seems fair to present two contrasting pictures. To support the conventional claim that no resemblance is intended to any living person, the central characters of these two sketches are known simply as A and B.

A is a Penal Therapy Officer, employed by the Community Control Service. A man in early middle age, respectably but not opulently dressed, his manner and expression signal a mixture of good intentions, anxiety and a certain habit of adjustment to frustration which mark him out as an experienced officer. Three or four years ago he passed the invisible barrier which separates promising (but slightly dangerous) youngsters from reliable (but unoriginal) 'backbone of the service' types, and he is now so firmly fixed in the latter position that he is never likely to be promoted. Consequently, he has in recent months become prone to moments of reflection on the nature and prospects of the service in which he is likely to spend another 15 years as a basic grade practitioner. These reflections tend to be more worrying than conclusive, and he normally escapes from them quickly into the day-to-day business of the job. He is doing so this morning, as he negotiates the electrically locked door of the large office block where he works, exchanges a few words with the general office staff and confronts the contents of his in-tray.

These are not untypical — messages relating to calls received while he was out; a reminder about overdue statistics; eight requests for 'correctional assessments' (which he still thinks of as social inquiry reports) for next week's court; a sharp note pointing out that he must not park his car in spaces reserved for police officers; and a circular from the Chief Community Control Officer informing him that applications for car loans will only be considered in future in respect of vehicles which conform to the new approved colour scheme for service vehicles. (This is rumoured to be blue with a faint pink stripe down the side.) He selects out those items needing immediate attention and settles down to sorting out the overdue caseload statistics.

As he does so, he reflects that he is really quite lucky to have entered the service at a time when the majority of recruits still received a social casework training. It is to this that he owes his status as a therapy officer, and because of this status nearly 20 per cent of his caseload are subject to supervision and control orders which allow him some scope and discretion in the guidance he gives them about their social difficulties (provided of course that he adheres to normal reporting frequencies and breach guidelines). He realises that this kind of work is increasingly regarded as an anachronism, and many of his colleagues are 'community control assistants' of various grades, responsible for supervising the office 'surveillance list' of post-custodial licences, partial release cases, Day Containment orders, night restriction orders, weekend restrictions and community service labour gangs. However, only four-fifths of his own case allocation is drawn from the surveillance list, and the remaining fifth represents, for him, the real core of his job.

This personal caseload gives him a chance to develop a close and, hopefully, helpful relationship with a few people early in their criminal careers with only one or two offences recorded against them. He feels there is still some prospect of influencing them away from the further crimes that will otherwise move them, step by step, through the various categories of community surveillance and on into custody. Sadly, many of them frustrate his good intentions, either reoffending or inviting breach proceedings through their occasional failure to report. In the old days, when breach action was more discretionary, he often took risks in overlooking technical failures, but since the development of computerised monitoring of records and the automatic initiation of breach proceedings this is not so easy to manage. In any case, many of his colleagues welcome the new system of automatic breach, seeing it as fairer overall even if its consequences seem harsh in some cases.

Most crime, he feels, stems from personal inadequacies which are not amenable to the kind of help he can provide (he has heard of a book by a psychologist which says something like this) and he is on the whole glad that the system allows him to be very selective in building up his personal caseload, though he wishes the other four-fifths of his allocation could be reduced somewhat. This would allow him more time to get at the underlying problems in those cases where there is a real opportunity for counselling and therapeutic work. Some of his clients could, he feels, make real strides towards maturity and a realistic acceptance of authority if only he could find time to get through to them.

Over the years he has become used to the chores which

get in the way of the 'real' work, but today he is particularly aware of this problem. As well as the statistics, he has three correctional assessments to finish before lunch; luckily, in two cases the agency already has comprehensive files which provide all the information for the assessment form without the need for a time-consuming interview with the defendant. The third one also turns out fairly straightforward: a visit to the police cells and a 20-minute chat cover the ground adequately. The defendant is quite upset, and insists that he would not be stealing if he had a job, but A quickly recognises this as a rationalisation (after all, unemployment is a predicament shared by five or six million others, and they do not all steal). In any case, the man has several previous convictions, and in these days of objective assessments and computer-assisted sentencing the outcome is predictably custodial. Remembering recent comments from the chief constable about 'unrealistically lenient' recommendations in correctional assessments, A, who believes in being honest, explains that his report will have to be realistic, but that some help may be available on an after-care basis. Unfortunately, the man becomes abusive and threatening, and the interview ends on a rather sour note. Afterwards, A feels that in a way his assessment is confirmed by this impulsive behaviour: clearly this man would not be easy to treat.

Lunch is a simple affair of sandwiches in the office while he finishes off the three assessment forms. Then, after a quick look at the newspaper ('Economic Recovery Just Around The Corner, Says Prime Minister'), it is time for the weekly staff meeting, which promises to be livelier than usual. The main item on the agenda is a discussion of a new policy document from the Correctional Administration Division of the Home Office, on which comments from various services are being invited. The proposal is that the community control service and the prison service should, within the next few years, become a unified Correctional Service, and the office team, in a rare gesture of democracy, has been asked to give its views for the benefit of senior management.

As the senior community control officer outlines the proposal, A finds himself becoming increasingly uneasy. Apparently the disappointingly low success rate of day containment orders, now producing a reconviction rate of 52 per cent within one year of sentence, is one of a number of factors influencing the Government towards still greater investment in the prison building programme and a doubling of the number of Secure Treatment Centres, which are currently overcrowded with recidivist offenders. A remembers that on recent visits to these centres he has been appalled not only by the overcrowding but also by the general atmosphere and regime; disturbances and minor riots are frequent, and when conditions are calm enough for him to interview prisoners he often finds them listless and confused, which they say is a result of the drugs they are required to take. Oddly, the same prisoners are described to him by secure treatment staff as adapting well, or 'making a positive response to behaviour modification'. A does not really welcome the prospect of closer involvement in the work of these centres, but it seems that within the proposed correctional service he could well find himself posted to one. He feels a little guilty at not seeing such a prospect as a challenge to his professionalism.

Meanwhile, his community control assistant colleagues seem mainly concerned about the implications for pay and conditions — will they become entitled to shift allowances and overtime payments like secure treatment staff? Nobody seems to know. The staff who run the Day Containment Unit in the office basement, and see themselves as a rather special group, point out that the reconviction figures are an unfair test of their work since most of their offenders already have convictions before entering the unit, and they cannot achieve much with them. They repeat their familiar argument that more day containment orders on first offenders, allowing them to make an impact earlier in criminal careers, would give them a better chance of success. A has always been puzzled about this, since nearly half the convictions relate to the offence of failing to comply with the conditions of day containment orders, and surely the regime bears some responsibility for this? No, say his colleagues from the Unit; discipline and credibility are vital parts of the containment process. On the whole, this group supports the proposed merger, as they feel it will make their law enforcement role clearer. They also feel they have a good deal to learn from their colleagues in Secure Treatment.

The three penal therapy officers in the team clearly have more reservations, and A feels impelled to act as their spokesman: 'Well . . . er . . . I think it's a very interesting proposal . . . but doesn't it rather conflict with the traditional ethos of our service? After all, we are basically a social work service . . .' 'Used to be, you mean', mutters somebody. A tries again: 'I mean, I realise it's all basically the same job, but surely we represent different attitudes, a different way of doing things. Would it really be in our interests to be merged with the prison service and Secure Treatment?' 'What about the possible advantages?' says somebody else, and the discussion returns to pay and conditions, the benefits of larger units in a climate of spending cuts, and so on. Gradually the staff meeting drifts into more practical matters of office administration, and A's attention wanders. He feels vaguely frustrated that he did not produce more positive, convincing arguments, but then he never claimed to be a theorist, and at least it was probably healthy to express his feelings. In any case, the real decisions will be taken somewhere else and perhaps the job will not really change that much.

After the staff meeting, he has visits to make. He hands his three assessment report forms to the junior assistant who does court duty, and sets off through the littered streets to the car park. On the way he passes a group of obviously unemployed youths being escorted, in handcuffs, towards the police station, the aftermath of another street disturbance. He is relieved to see that their injuries seem fairly minor. More customers for Day Containment and Secure Treatment. A young policeman asks to see his identity card — 'Just a routine check, sir' — luckily he has it with him. 'Penal Therapy, is it, sir? What do you think about this lot, then?' But experience has taught him ways of avoiding this kind of conversation, and soon he is on his way.

And at this point we must leave him. We have shared enough of his day to form some ideas of the man and his job, and we cannot judge him harshly — he is kind, he means well, he is liked by most of his clients, all the clerical staff, many of his colleagues and some of his managers. He did not create the social world he works in, and he does the best he can in the small space left to him. His ideas and theories about his job are well adapted to this small space, which is best defined by the notion of marginality — the criminal justice system rolls on its punitive way, and his activities have no observable effect on it. The unofficial self-help organisations and claimants' groups (which are beginning to attend the courts and offer a kind of supportive supervision for offenders in return for a conditional discharge) do not invite him to their meetings, and he would probably regard them as unprofessional and rather suspect anyway. One grain of comfort is that the threat to his job may be less than it seems, since a highly coercive system often looks better with a frill of token welfare round the edges, and this is just what A provides.

For our contrasting glimpse of a different possible future, we return to the same time and much the same place, but presuppose a rather different history.

B is a Community Probation Officer. Like many of his colleagues in a service still undergoing modest expansion, he is fairly young, well educated, not spectacularly well paid but very interested in the job. We join him as he arrives at his local court and, after a quick visit to the cells to see if any familiar faces have found their way there overnight, he takes his place at the probation desk in the courtroom. A brief exchange of comments with some of the duty solicitors and the voluntary victim advocate is interrupted by the entry of the magistrates, and the court gets down to business. B already has some knowledge of several of the cases, but others on the list are new to him.

The first case concerns three young men who pleaded guilty to a burglary two weeks ago, and were adjourned for reports to determine whether appropriate programmes of supervision were available in the community. All three have a record, and one comes from a home where the service has been involved for several years. B has reports on all three, which cover their background, the circumstances of the joint offence, and the discussions which have taken place with the defendants about possible programmes which might be useful to them as well as constituting an adequate offer to the court. He has also just received a brief note about the victim, prepared by the local victim support scheme, which among other things details the damage done and indicates that the victim (a woman living on her own) would be happy to have the damage repaired by the offenders provided that they were properly supervised and she did not have to meet them. The court asks for comments from the victim advocate, who points out that the victim has preferred not to attend the hearing but seems quite willing to be involved in this way in any programme for the offenders. B then suggests that this element could be built into a programme of supervision for two of the defendants, but supervision of the work will be difficult unless the victim support scheme can offer somebody. The victim advocate, who also helps to run the support scheme, indicates with some satisfaction that this will be no problem, and B suggests that the remainder of the supervision programme could be as outlined in the reports.

The third defendant presents more of a problem, as he has a more serious record and was already on probation when the offence occurred. He also has the opportunity of a job, but this involves moving away from the area. B welcomes this as a colleague has been trying for some time to help this young man find work and reasonable accommodation away from a very difficult home, and some useful programmes are available under a probation order in his new area, but he would not be in a position to do any work for the victim. He explains the situation to the magistrates, who ask the defendants if they have anything to add and then retire to consider what to do. Quite quickly they emerge; they are prepared to make probation orders on the first two defendants, on condition that the suggested programme is followed, including necessary repairs to the victim's house. The orders are formally explained; the defendants, B and the victim advocate formally agree and the defendants are instructed to wait outside until B has a chance to see them. In the third case, the magistrates have some reservations but have decided to defer sentence for three months, with a view to making a new probation order if reports on progress in the new area are satisfactory and some compensation is paid.

B is on the whole quite pleased with this outcome. He would have liked the reparation condition not to be formally written into the orders, as he prefers simple orders and knows that extra conditions will be regarded as further up the tariff; but the Clerk to the Justices regards the formal condition as a necessary safeguard for the victim, and B knows that the victim advocate, a formidable lady, agrees with this view. Realistically, B does not expect to have things all his own way, and a readiness to accept this kind of condition in a probation order seems a fair price for the goodwill of the local victim support scheme.

He has time to give the three men some basic information about where to report to join an induction group for their probation, and to check that they fully understand what they have agreed to do, while the court deals with some minor offences by way of compensation orders and conditional discharges. A more serious case comes next: a man has stolen a fairly large number of video recorders from a warehouse with the intention of reselling them, and nearly got away with what was a fairly well-planned scheme. This is a new case for B, and he does not know the man; the magistrates clearly regard the offence seriously, although the duty solicitor points out that there was no direct personal victim. They adjourn the case for reports, indicating that a custodial sentence is possible, and B makes a careful note of this so that the officer producing the report will realise that any alternative suggestion will need to be argued carefully. He knows there probably will be some alternative offered, as service policy discourages the practice of recommending custodial sentences, and inconclusive reports are also discouraged by a process of screening in the team before they reach the court.

And so the morning goes on, with some cases ending well from B's point of view, some less well. A young man who injured a stranger in a pub fight, not for the first time, receives a custodial sentence, but as he has a job the court accepts a suggestion that he serve it in the form of weekend imprisonment, which will also enable him to pay compensation from his wages. In another case, a tactical error nearly brings about a bad result: an enthusiastic volunteer member of the new local Mediation Project has secured what looks like a voluntary compensation agreement between offender and victim but has done so before the court has had an opportunity to consider the case at all, rather than following the more usual course of arranging a discussion during an adjournment for reports. The magistrates are clearly annoyed, feeling that they are being manipulated, and the victim advocate, ever alert for signs of undue pressure on victims, suggests that the discussion may have been rushed. Sensing that this muddle might tip the scales towards an unusually heavy fine on an unemployed man, B suggests that if the magistrates wish to adjourn for a report, he can also talk to the people involved and check if the agreement was arrived at in a reasonable way. They accept this, and B makes a note to check whether the Mediation Project has discussed procedures fully with the court.

By the end of the court sitting, B has collected rather more work than he hoped, but has been able to intervene usefully in a number of cases. For the second time this week the court has made far more probation orders than community service orders, and he wonders if it is time the community service team arranged another tour of their projects for interested magistrates. On the way out of the court, he meets one of the senior magistrates and remembers to ask if he is available for next week's meeting of the Probation Development Group, which is trying to initiate a wider range of practical programmes for inclusion in probation orders for more serious offenders. This particular magistrate knows a number of local employers well, and the group hopes that he may persuade some of them to co-operate in a work experience scheme.

Much of B's job, in fact, consists of this kind of formal and informal liaison with a variety of local figures and community organisations of all kinds, trying to fit them and the needs of his agency's clients together. He is a pragmatist and opportunist, enjoying the bustle and variety, but often wishes he could spend more time with his individual clients. He still does a good deal of this kind of work — yesterday, for instance, he spent much of the evening exploring problems and possible solutions with a very depressed and unhappy man who had done so much shoplifting that the authorities, in desperation, had at last prosecuted him. He sees some of his clients very regularly for counselling, but with others his main work is concentrated around social inquiry, the negotiation of appropriate programmes, the exploration of problems in an induction group or the search for alternatives when something goes wrong. Much of the day-to-day supervision of his clients is undertaken by a variety of volunteers or voluntary organisations who offer different kinds of

service. These have developed rapidly now that many
people are taking the option of a four-day week and
spending the extra day in a range of (on the whole) useful
activities. (He often wonders about doing this himself, but
on the whole enjoys full-time work, and needs a full
salary.) Part of his job is to monitor the quality of work
done with probation clients by the independent bodies, to
encourage the good ones and to help in development
work. Some of his colleagues worry about 'deprofessional-
isation', but he knows something about the track record
of the welfare professions and is prepared to try almost
anything which seems likely to be effective. He feels he
has a caseload of volunteers (often themselves former
offenders), projects, little organisations and referral
systems as well as of clients, and he keeps notes and
records on them in the same way, discussing their progress
with supervisors and colleagues. Several times he has
asked for more policy guidance on his dealings with the
community, since sometimes he makes enemies as well as
friends for the agency, but his managers have now
admitted that policy in this area needs clarifying and have
asked him to draft a set of guidelines, so he half wishes he
had not raised the matter.

Lunch turns into an informal meeting, as he has
arranged to have a pint with the police sergeant
responsible for the police version of community liaison.
As this officer also sits on the Mediation Project
committee, B talks about the problem in court that
morning. Apparently the committee has tried to persuade
volunteers to use consistent procedures, but some
volunteers are impatient with what they see as bureaucracy
and the committee does not want to discourage them
through too much rigidity. B wonders if one way to
approach this might be to ask a sympathetic magistrate to
lead a discussion with the volunteer group about courts
and sentencing, and the sergeant agrees to pursue this in
the committee. Resisting the temptation of a further pint,
they set off for their various afternoon duties — the

sergeant to a Juvenile Crime Prevention Panel meeting, and B to his office team meeting, for which he is only five minutes late.

The meeting has just started, and his lateness evokes only a brief sigh from his senior officer, a tolerant man who leads by example rather than direct control. The staff meeting is chaired by all officers in turn, and its function is to review team activity and any new ideas advanced by members in relation to team objectives. Today the atmosphere is optimistic, as the office microcomputer has shown a 10 per cent decline in custodial sentencing in the local criminal justice system over the last six months; however, two members of the team have made an analysis of the offenders still receiving custodial sentences, and some of them are clearly people for whom a convincing pattern of supervision has not yet been developed. These officers express an interest in developing something, and are asked to prepare proposals for the next meeting; the usual pattern is that proposals which convince most of the team will be accepted and implemented, but will then be monitored to ensure that they demonstrate effectiveness in terms of team and agency objectives. In the light of the discussion, a target of a further 12 per cent reduction is accepted as realistic for the next six months.

Members then report on new developments (some good, some bad) in their current areas of activity, and the three officers who run the probation induction process report on new probationers so that decisions can be made about their allocation within or outside the team. Basic objectives are quickly noted for each client, and these will be fed into the computer-aided case review system, which also now reminds them of overdue reviews on seven other clients. These are allocated, a few other routine items are dealt with, and the meeting moves on to the major item of new business.

This is a contentious proposal from a county working party on decentralisation, which has come up with the idea that the probation team should disperse into smaller units which would be accommodated in small 'patch' offices in areas of high need, possibly sharing with the recently decentralised local authority social work teams. (These still have considerable involvement with many offenders' families despite the gradual transfer of most juvenile supervision work back to the probation service.) Such an arrangement, it is argued, would make officers more accessible and promote better liaison with other services. Team responses are varied; some officers, particularly those with an interest in neighbourhood community development, are enthusiastic, while others, including B, believe that the process of influencing the criminal justice system requires good access to courts and all the associated agencies, which their present site provides. Some of the specialists in individual counselling and group programmes are worried about the practicality of group induction and properly planned packages if the team is geographically fragmented, and the issue is clearly going to be difficult to resolve. In the end, the team agrees to follow up B's idea of surveying the views of existing clients, magistrates and voluntary organisations as well as social workers, to find out which arrangement they would see as most likely to improve effectiveness. This will take a few weeks, and a date is set for discussion at a future meeting.

This concludes the business, and B, wondering slightly whether he is wise to have taken on yet another task, spends a necessary hour on rapid paperwork and recording before setting off on a round of visits. These include not only clients but a couple of small voluntary organisations which may be able to offer something, and a discussion with the local public prosecutor's office about whether the probation service can offer or facilitate any programmes which might be usable by their staff as alternatives to prosecution. B is in principle in favour of this, but anxious to avoid any confusion between what might be available on a voluntary basis to a cautioned offender and the more

demanding and substantial packages available as alternatives to custodial sentences. There is also the problem
of resources, but he thinks a project of this kind might be
eligible for grant aid from the new National Crime
Prevention Commission.

And so his day goes on. It will be clear by now that his
job is demanding, making substantial claims on his energy,
his social work skills and many other abilities, and he is
not always successful; however, he enjoys using his own
initiative and is encouraged to do so provided he can
demonstrate progress in terms of agency and team
objectives. Luckily he has had some training in community
development and basic research techniques as well as
more traditional social work skills, and he has a good
knowledge of the criminal justice system supported by
reasonably efficient information technology. He wishes
that more of the 'packages' he arranges for clients could
be bridges to permanent employment, but this is still a
scarce opportunity despite the progress of job-sharing and
part-time work schemes. His team is understaffed, as
growth in workload has tended to outstrip growth in
agency resources, and now that most of the easier target
groups are regularly diverted from custodial sentences the
remainder present more of a challenge. He spends slightly
less time than he used to on direct work with clients and
regrets this, but his service development activities produce
a measurable degree of success and this maintains his
commitment, enthusiasm and preparedness to take risks.
Every two years he is entitled to a three-month sabbatical
for further training or study, either with the local university
or at the National Probation Development Institute, and
he usually comes back from these with some new ideas.

But we must abandon this tempting fantasy and return
to the present. We have seen both A and B at work, and
how different they are. They also, of course, have much
in common which has not been emphasised in our brief
spying: both are genuinely concerned for their clients
most of the time, both are social workers at heart, both

are familiar with the draining effect of constant exposure to other people's problems and unhappiness, both know the difficulty of starting again after failure and frustration. Given different circumstances, perhaps either of them could come to resemble the other; but as we have encountered them, the main danger to B is that he will burn himself out through trying to use all the opportunities open to him, and his managers should sometimes encourage him to slow down. A, on the other hand, glows so faintly that he is hardly visible. Contextual differences are also important: social workers do not operate in a political vacuum, and the two scenarios presuppose rather different histories of political and social development. A's world is characterised by an authoritarian and coercive approach to social problems, and B would find it more difficult to operate in such a climate; his work involves a respect for the value and rights of citizens and a commitment to their welfare in a more libertarian and participatory society than A's, and these differences would also be reflected in wider economic and social policies which lie outside the concerns of this book. What distinguishes their different approaches to their daily work is partly history and partly agency policy, but mainly a radically different view of their possible contribution to developing a more acceptable and humane system of criminal justice. What can we learn from them about today's problems?

10

Enhanced Probation and Alternatives to Custody

To return from the problems of an imagined future to those of the present, I have tried to suggest and illustrate the possibility that social work services in the criminal justice system should be concerned as much about their influence on that system as about their effects on individual clients. In policy and practical decisions about how, and in what directions, to exercise that influence, the following principles seem to be important:

1 *Maximum feasible voluntarism* The attempt to reduce coercion in criminal justice is partly an ethical principle, based on a conception of man (or woman) as an active subject, a participant or potential participant in the creation of his or her circumstances and social world. It is a libertarian and humanistic notion, honoured in principle by the ideology of democratic societies even if often absent in their practice. It also commands considerable empirical support: decision-making in criminal justice need not be as coercive as in our system, and often is not. On purely utilitarian grounds an increasing body of social work research suggests that people are more likely to change their behaviour, or to be helped to change it, when the process of change can enlist their co-operation by reflecting their own goals and choices.

2 *Maximum feasible participation* The opportunity to exercise choices and to participate in decisions which directly affect us is another aspect of the same humanistic principle. We have a right to be involved where our

interests or welfare are at stake, and we are likely to feel dissatisfied when decisions are made about us through procedures which pay no attention to our perceptions and aspirations. Respect for persons implies negotiation rather than manipulation. Again, there are good reasons to believe that the goals of criminal justice can often be pursued more effectively in this way, but this is not to argue that participation is desirable on purely instrumental grounds, to help to achieve the system's aims; on the contrary, it should itself be one of those aims, since the system should seek to produce outcomes that reflect the interests and needs of those involved. This applies in principle to victims as much as to offenders.

3 *Recognition of responsibility* To the extent that offences result from voluntary choice and do harm, recognition of the offender's humanity implies recognition of his accountability. Demands made on offenders by the criminal justice system should be proportionate to their responsibility for harm, and should reflect moral evaluations of the seriousness of the act; they should also, as far as possible, recognise personal responsibility by creating opportunities for practical or symbolic undoing of the harm. The *extent* of demands made (that is, the extent to which the offender's future choices are constrained as a consequence of past acts) should reflect principles of proportionate justice in relation to moral judgements of seriousness. The *manner* in which demands are to be met should be, as far as possible, negotiated and agreed.

4 *Social justice* The recognition of personal responsibility does not mean that *only* personal responsibility should be recognised. People may be able to choose how they respond to the world, but they do not usually choose the world in which they have to respond. Lack of legitimate resources, opportunities and power may figure as large in the experience of many offenders as it does in the lives of some of their victims, and offers of help are justified by the need for help rather than by the fact of offending. As social actors we do not start equal, and it is

not fair or realistic to expect some offenders not to offend unless their opportunities to survive without crime are improved. These considerations should also affect our moral judgements on their acts. Historically, our criminal justice system has often confused or obscured these realities: the same politicians who stress law and order and the personal wickedness of offenders pursue economic policies which increase poverty and inequality, and perpetuate the entrapment of many offenders in a deprived underclass where the realities of daily experience encourage crime. The dramatic labelling and scapegoating of individual offenders has the ideological effect of diverting our attention from our collective responsibility for conditions in which the rewards of *not* offending may be hardly worth having. Unfortunately, as Lea and Young (1984) point out, the traditional left's emphasis on the social causes of crime and the attempt to play down the offender's personal responsibility for harm constitute an equally unrealistic denial of problems and a disservice to victims. A criminal justice system which ignores crime would not be particularly useful, but one in which the moral basis for decisions was explicit and open to discussion could be extremely useful. It is doubtful if any criminal justice system can be a strong force for social change, but one based on more realistic evaluations of personal and social responsibility could help to stimulate a more progressive debate on the politics of crime. This raises issues of more general policy which go beyond the scope of this book; but any attempt at a more consistent approach to questions of seriousness and responsibility must lead us to ask how far the commercially motivated display techniques of supermarkets facilitate shoplifting, why cheating Social Security out of a few pounds is taken so much more seriously than cheating Inland Revenue out of thousands, and many other similar questions.

5 *Creativity* This seems almost too obvious to merit inclusion, but we often seem to expect clients to adapt themselves to services rather than the other way round.

The literature provides examples of elaborate attempts to persuade clients, against their better judgements, that their problems really are of the kind that the agency prefers to deal with (e.g. Mayer and Timms 1970; Smith 1980). The continuous adaptation and innovation needed in revising services to meet client need and agency objectives is a challenge, which in our futuristic fable was accepted by officer B but not by officer A. Social work services in the criminal justice system would, if they follow the objectives outlined above, need to be creative in their approach not only to methods of work with existing clients, but to the needs of clients who do not yet come their way; to the perceived needs of sentencers; to systems of liaison, gatekeeping, referral and allocation; and to the process of influencing other organisations, other professionals and the community at large.

6 *Effectiveness* The only way to make such a large task manageable would be by continuous testing of innovations and proposed innovations in relation to agency objectives, and the adoption of an agreed system of priorities. This has been recognised by the Home Office in its recent *Statement of National Objectives and Priorities* for the probation service (Home Office 1984), and although that document can be criticised in its details the principle seems unquestionable. However, objectives and creativity by themselves do not guarantee effectiveness. There are many service innovations, described as 'experiments', which are in fact merely changes; they do not become experiments until their outcomes are measured and tested against their original intentions, as a guide to decisions about whether to go on, stop, or go somewhere else. The issue was clearly stated by the Seebohm Committee: 'It is both wasteful and irresponsible to set experiments in motion and omit to record and analyse what happens. It makes no sense in terms of administrative efficiency and, however little intended, it indicates a careless attitude towards human welfare' (Seebohm 1968). This remains sound advice, and perhaps the results of the

committee's activities continue to demonstrate their point. The aspiration to evaluate is not enough: the skills and the data must be there too.

So much for principles: their test is in their application. They are useful if they reduce uncertainty in decision-making while still enabling good decisions to be made. Do they throw any light on current problems of policy and practice in the provision of social work services for offenders? To explore this, we can return to some of the issues raised in chapter 3 where we explored a number of rival prescriptions for the future of social work with offenders.

The underlying question at that stage of our enquiry seemed to be: should we concentrate on providing help for offenders, or on meeting the expressed need of the criminal justice system for a range of non-custodial punishments? This issue has been sharpened by the 1982 Criminal Justice Act which allows for the strengthening of probation orders by the inclusion of a wide range of additional positive and negative requirements, and by the Home Office statement of priorities which gives pride of place to diversion: 'The first priority should be to ensure that, wherever possible, offenders can be dealt with by non-custodial measures and that standards of supervision are set and maintained at the level required for this purpose.' This involves 'maintaining the confidence of the courts in the ability of non-custodial measures to cope with a wide range of offenders'. Attitudes within the service range from the enthusiasm of a minority of agency managers for control, containment and deterrence to a marked scepticism among many officers (e.g. Drakeford 1983) about the use of any additional requirements in probation orders to create diversionary programmes. Additional requirements, they argue, transform probation from a kind of liberty into a kind of containment; they raise the possibility of oversurveillance and increased breach rates; they risk locating probation too high up the tariff ladder, and acting as an accelerated route into custody; and there is no way of guaranteeing that they will be used in a truly diversionary way. The route to diversion lies through limiting the punitive powers of sentencers, not through changing the behaviour of probation officers away from their traditional ethos. Nonsense, say their opponents: traditional probation orders have failed to divert because courts no longer regard them as appropriate for the more serious offender; our political system resists limitations on the powers of sentencers, and the 1982 Act actually increases them, so the only available route to diversion is by increasing the credible options available to the courts; probation should move up the tariff ladder, and good professional practice could ensure that strengthened probation orders are reserved for offenders who are not likely to receive ordinary probation orders; if we take diversion seriously then extra conditions in probation orders are necessary, and philosophical arguments about liberty and containment are not a proper occupation for practical men. The major obstacle is seen as the resistance of some (presumably immature) officers to the elements of authority and control which are inherent in their function.

Such a divisive issue cries out for a principled and empirical exploration. First, it should be recognised that there is some justice on both sides. Certainly shorter statutory limits on prison sentences would do more to empty the prisons than even a large amount of diversionary probation, and the fact that every recent attempt to do this has been frustrated by the political resistance of sentencers to executive interference does not reduce its desirability, only its feasibility. Past attempts at diversionary legislation *have* tended to fail: suspended sentences were used largely for offenders who would not have gone to prison anyway in the absence of the power to suspend, and some of them eventually served longer sentences than they would otherwise have done when they reoffended during suspension. Intermediate treatment developed largely as a voluntary extra resource for minor offenders and non-offenders rather than as a diversion from residential care and custody, and its use in this way probably accelerated the system's custodial drift. Even community service, a striking success in most ways, seems to be used instead of a prison sentence only about half the time. However, we can go further than acknowledging a few palpable hits on each side. If the arguments advanced in this book have any validity, it should be possible to offer both diversion and help, and to do so in ways which do not involve much trading off of one against the other, by applying principles consistent with those outlined above.

If we ignore for the time being the matter of extra conditions and consider initially the prior question of eligibility for probation itself, the principles of reducing coercion and increasing participation suggest an approach based on a combined assessment of opportunities for diversion and opportunities for help. This is illustrated schematically in figure 2. Only the top two cells of the

NEED FOR HELP

		High	Low	
	High	1 Eligible	2 ?	} Diversion
RISK OF CUSTODY				
	Low	3 ?	4 Not eligible	

Figure 2   Eligibility for probation

diagram represent diversion. Bearing in mind that we are looking for principles to guide agencies in what offers they might make to sentencers rather than laying down sentencing guidelines, the eligibility of offenders in the top left-hand category 1, who combine a need for help with a need for diversion, would command a good deal of support; the practical problem is to make a convincing enough case for probation here to satisfy sentencers' perceptions of seriousness. The upper right-hand group 2, comprising offenders with whom it is difficult to develop any agreed programme for help but who might be diverted from custody, presents a different problem. The aim of reducing coercion through diversion away from custody may suggest a role here for 'reporting only' orders: in 'sentenced to social work' terms (Bryant et al. 1978) these would be orders based on the primary legal contract only, without a subsidiary social work agreement. Such offenders could also be candidates for programmes such as community service which aim at useful outcomes for others rather than help for the offender. However, the danger is that we could come to see *all* diversion as relating to situation 2: hence the temptation to set up packages simply on the basis of their presumed attractiveness to sentencers, with only peripheral or marginal consideration of offenders' needs and how they might be helped. Thus 'controlism' tends to assimilate category 1 to category 2 and the problems and opportunities of helping are squeezed out.

An approach more in keeping with the principle of participation could be, in effect, to offer provisions for category 2 which maximise their chances of assimilation to category 1 by ensuring that full opportunities are available for making informed choices about possible help. If we regard category 1 as offering the optimum combination of help and diversion, this suggests that patterns of probation designed to extend into category 2 should meet at least the following criteria:

1 They should be significantly less coercive than the custody they are intended to replace.
2 They should be offered only on the basis of the client's fully informed consent rather than on a 'take it or leave it' basis.

3　Programmes should be flexible enough to allow some negotiation and client choice about how demands should be met, rather than totally pre-determined.

4　Both induction into a programme and its continuing implementation should include substantial opportunities for probationers to explore problems, assess their situation, consider realistic possibilities of help relating to agreed difficulties, and enter into negotiated commitments of this kind if they wish.

Obviously such criteria would have implications for the design and staffing of any form of probation specifically aimed at category 2. On the other hand, they also suggest that if programmes are designed to offer these opportunities, they will begin to look very like the sort of programme which would make sense for category 1. This is because the principle of participation in decisions suggests that even arrangements for category 1 should include opportunities for probationers to refuse some kinds of help without putting themselves at risk in terms of compliance with the primary legal contract. Thus the policy of developing non-custodial community punishments, designed specifically for category 2 offenders on the assumption that help is irrelevant, may be a blind alley. If arrangements are made instead on the assumption that any provision made under a probation order should include opportunities to negotiate help, including the opportunity not to be helped provided that the legal contract is honoured, then there seems no logical reason why category 2 could not be flexibly accommodated within arrangements designed as vehicles for both help and diversion rather than for diversion alone.

Category 3, where there is a basis for agreed help but no significant diversionary effect, is a category in which many probation orders have been made. However, the risk of putting too many eggs in this particular basket is that probation could come to be seen as non-diversionary in intent, and might also subject some offenders to greater legal constraints on their liberty than if they had received a sentence commensurate simply with the perceived seriousness of the offence. The danger of blurring and net-widening, of extending paternalistic social controls on 'welfare' grounds to people who would be less severely handled on 'justice' grounds, is relevant here; and while the principle of voluntarism suggests that the option of probation should be available it also suggests that where people are prepared to enter into negotiated agreements about help independently of a legal contract they should have the opportunity to do precisely that. In other words, a preferred option to explore in these circumstances might be to offer help on a voluntary basis, perhaps combined with a conditional discharge, if the seriousness of the act does not warrant the legal restrictions of a probation order. The traditional view that the legal requirements of probation might be justified not by the seriousness of the offence but by their effectiveness in persuading reluctant clients to accept help now seems difficult to advance: it cannot be supported on moral grounds, since it involves injustice, and the empirical evidence is also against it, since although the legal requirements are enforceable no corresponding guarantees can be given about the effectiveness of the help.

If a policy of offering voluntary help to low-tariff offenders were followed, it could well increase diversionary opportunities for other offenders by heightening the perceived seriousness of probation; however, much thought would be needed about how to weigh such work in officers' workloads and what priority to allocate to it. It is difficult to avoid the conclusion that with limited resources, work which combines help with diversion should have a higher priority than work which does not; on the other hand, this does involve selectivity about which needs will be met. Such considerations are already looming large in discussions about the future resources available to the probation service; for instance, the Home Office view of priorities has been criticised for under-emphasising voluntary after-care and work around the civil courts where much useful help can be and has been provided. However, if influencing the criminal justice system is accepted as a major objective of services undertaking social work with offenders, this cannot but affect the priority given to work which has different objectives.

Category 4, where neither help nor diversion is on the agenda, seems uncontroversial; most would agree that the appropriate outcomes here do not include probation. Such orders may be made by accident or through the uncertainties inherent in the social inquiry process, but they would generally be regarded as anomalies and as good candidates for early termination or conversion into conditional discharges.

Such a framework for considering eligibility for probation illustrates ways in which practical choices could be influenced by the kind of principles outlined early in the chapter. Although the discussion has concentrated on probation orders, much the same logic could be applied to juvenile supervision orders and other attempts by social work agencies to provide diversionary services in the context of criminal justice. An extension of the same arguments suggests a possible approach to the question of additional requirements in orders, and under what conditions they could reasonably be used. To argue that they should *never* be used invites collusion with a sentencing pattern which uses probation mainly in category 3 and does not divert; on the other hand, to envisage them as the *standard* form of future probation orders risks excessive intervention in category 3 without guaranteeing diversionary effectiveness in categories 1 and 2. In reality it appears that the opponents of additional conditions are prepared to accept some of them (they have not, to my knowledge, campaigned for the abolition of conditions of residence in probation hostels); the real questions are how far and when they should be used.

A fairly strict application of the suggested logic of eligibility would suggest that extra conditions can be useful, but should not be encouraged unless they meet at least the following criteria:

1 Extra demands should reflect the greater perceived seriousness of the offence. That is, enhanced probation orders should be explicitly located above normal probation in the tariff scale, without displacing normal probation or other non-custodial options downwards.

2 The extra demands should form a framework within which help could be provided. They should not be simply punitive or deterrent in intent.

3 Any programme created around the extra demands should offer opportunities for help of a reasonably effective kind, relating to problems defined as far as possible through joint assessments by professional staff and clients.

4 Additional conditions should be negotiated and agreed in advance, with a high degree of client participation.

5 All programmes set up on the basis of additional conditions should be regularly evaluated to determine whether in practice they conform to these criteria. This seems to be vital, as all diversionary programmes are operating against some of the inherent pressures of the criminal justice system and some degree of drift away from original objectives and intended target groups is likely to be normal rather than exceptional. Only careful evaluation can identify such drift and create opportunities for its prevention. This also suggests that evaluation strategies must incorporate a falsification principle: that is, they must be capable of identifying not only evidence that a project works, but also evidence

that it does not work. The adequacy of a project's design to meet its objectives provides only a limited protection against drift; it also needs an adequate evaluation strategy, which is an area of neglect in many recent 'experiments'.

Real life, of course, is not so tidy; judgements are made in shades of grey and matters of degree and no neat system of categories and criteria will provide clear answers in situations where information is necessarily limited. This is particularly true of evaluation in diversionary projects. Many factors influence sentencing, and diversionary sentencing decisions are neither directly observable nor measurable; the particular reasons for individual sentencing decisions are locked away inside sentencers' heads, and may not be fully understood or accurately reported even by sentencers themselves. Nevertheless, much more could be attempted than is usually done to develop a range of indirect indicators of diversion, even with the information that agencies naturally collect in the course of their work.

It is possible, for instance, to monitor local sentencing trends over the life of a project or new pattern of service to determine whether custodial sentencing changes in a direction consistent with diversion. Local figures can be compared with the local sentencing baseline before the start of the project, and with figures from areas where the particular alternative in question is not available, or with national sentencing trends published in the annual volumes of *Criminal Statistics*. The level of *other non-custodial* sentences can also be monitored, in case a new project is diverting offenders not from custody but simply from 'normal' probation or from community service. The offending histories of those referred to the project can be compared with those receiving custodial sentences locally, or nationally as revealed in *Prison Statistics*, to determine whether they are offenders at a comparable, lower or indeed higher tariff level than those who normally receive custodial sentences. Reconviction and breach rates can tell us something about whether the project is putting offenders at greater risk of accelerating up the sentencing ladder, or the public at greater risk in comparison with reconviction rates following custodial sentences. Agencies will also hold data on what happens to those referred to the project if they subsequently breach requirements or reoffend.

Patterns of work within agencies, as measured for management purposes or statistical returns, will also often reveal something about referral systems, the screening of potential recruits to a project, or the extent to which work arising from custodial sentencing is being replaced by work arising from diversion. In fact, the information already available or fairly easily obtainable in an agency practising social work around the criminal justice system can provide a remarkably comprehensive picture of how that system is behaving and of the effects of any attempts to influence it. The process is, of course, much easier if an evaluation strategy is developed not as an afterthought but as an integral part of initial planning. Project objectives can then be expressed in a clear and testable form, and recording systems developed with evaluation in mind.

Evaluation can also to some extent address itself to the question of help. The difficulties are perhaps greater here: the data are 'softer' (though no less real or important) and the problems of gathering them without distorting or interfering with the day-to-day work are considerable. So are the dangers of observer bias when staff are involved in assessing their own project. However, where projects undertake systematic assessment of clients or record individual objectives it is possible to generate some useful measures without excessive distortion, and at least to learn more than is likely to emerge from purely impressionistic or intuitive evaluation. An interesting example is provided by the evaluation of the 'task-centred probation' experiment in London's Differential Treatment Unit (Goldberg and Stanley 1979) where the task-centred method required recording of agreed target problems and agreed tasks for each client. It was then possible to assess progress through the use of follow-up ratings by clients of the extent of problem alleviation, and by staff of the extent of task performance, drawing on procedures which were already part of the pattern of the work. This provided some information about the extent of changes in problems and of the success of the project in terms of objectives which clients had helped to define, as opposed to the more limited and perhaps less relevant measures provided by reconviction rates alone.

Other possibilities include straightforward consumer surveys (e.g. Davies 1979), though these tend to be time-consuming and often require the use of an independent researcher since responses given to project staff in positions of authority may be affected by that context. There is also the danger that they may tell us more about what people liked than about whether it was useful. Another possible approach, now that standardised check-lists of various kinds are often used in social work assessment, is to develop measures of progress through administration of questionnaires or checklists before and after involvement in a project. A variety of approaches are possible, and all can add something to our under-standing of the extent to which helpful intentions are actually achieved.

To illustrate the application in practice of the suggested criteria for enhanced probation, let us return again to chapter 3 and the issues raised by the Kent Probation Control Unit, contrasting it with a less well-known example of an arguably more successful enhanced probation project. In case it seems unfair or tendentious to single out the Kent unit again, it should be remembered that it was seen as representative of a possible trend, and it is to its credit that it has been sufficiently well documented, particularly in its aims and planning, to allow a critical examination which many other projects have avoided. Much of the original adverse reaction was intuitive, based on a perceived threat to traditional attitudes and on an emotional response to the rhetoric of control and discipline which accompanied the unit's introduction. Some criticisms also reflected a more empirical awareness of the problems of effective diversion and the risks of a regime based on increased surveillance without, apparently, a corresponding attention to needs and help. However, the unit's originality and ingenuity are hard to deny and it therefore offers a good test of the suggested criteria.

Clearly it was planned as a genuinely diversionary resource, and thus meets the first suggested requirement that enhanced probation should try to locate itself at a higher tariff level than 'normal' probation. However, the unit's rules and their reflection in additional requirements of probation orders stressed matters of discipline and restriction, and the rigidities of the programme, together with its administrative largely by ancillary grade staff, raise serious doubts about the extent to which it could accommodate a helping role in relation to a variety of needs. The cursory attention given in the planning documents to induction of clients into the project suggests little joint assessment of problems and of possible opportunities of help, and this raises doubts about how far the second and third of the suggested criteria for enhanced probation were met in practice. The fourth suggested requirement, relating to informed negotiation and agreement in advance, is harder to assess from the information available. Certainly there seems to be little space for negotiations about the content of the programme, and although consent was a legal requirement this must often have been given in the expectation that a custodial sentence would otherwise be imposed. This is a problem affecting consent in all diversionary schemes and reflects the fact that current sentencing practice does not usually offer offenders a clear choice between stated alternatives; however, to consent to daily containment and surveillance over many months, as clients of the unit had to, is a serious business and imposes on those negotiating such consent a heavy obligation to ensure that the project is as effectively diversionary as it is intended to be. Thus we return to the fifth requirement of effective evaluation: how far did the arrangements for such a unit incorporate procedures for self-evaluation and self-correction? Certainly it attempted to do so: an evaluation report on its first year was prepared and quite widely distributed (Kent Probation Service 1982). Evaluation over a longer period was frustrated by the unit's closure when the case of Cullen v. Rogers showed it to be illegal; however, the new provisions of the 1982 Criminal Justice Act permit its reactivation in a slightly modified form, so the evaluation is still relevant to a continuing project design. The report informs us, quite early on, that 'it is fair to conclude that those attending the PCU were indeed diverted from imprisonment'; but the nature of the evidence on which this conclusion is based must cast some doubt on the adequacy of the evaluation strategy to support it.

For instance, there is no analysis of sentencing trends to support the claim of effective diversion. Although evidence is presented on the offending histories of the first 22 clients, no attempt is made to compare these with the histories of those entering custody either locally or nationally. Without a sentencing analysis or a comparison of previous convictions it is virtually impossible to support diversionary claims. It is made clear that some clients of the unit were quite serious offenders; however, the report also shows that among those who were recommended for a place at the unit but were sentenced differently by the courts, over a third received non-custodial sentences while others (it is not clear how many) received prison sentences of a few months only, much shorter than the proposed period of attendance at the unit. Other parts of the report (including one on 'indiscipline and reoffending') provide interesting insights into the regime and the clients' experiences, and might help to allay some critics' fears of an unreasonably punitive atmosphere; however, overall evidence of effective diversion is thin. This is worrying in a project which laid such emphasis on containment and control, and justified this almost exclusively by reference to its diversionary aims.

Some other examples of enhanced probation in practice appear to demonstrate a more promising fit with the suggested criteria. The four experimental day training centres set up under the 1972 Criminal Justice Act, for instance, involved greater restrictions than a normal probation order; but they used the opportunities created by daily attendance to implement a variety of methods of joint assessment, and emphasised participation in programmes which were designed around offenders' needs (Vanstone 1985). The Government's decision not to develop the day training centre model probably reflected consideration of cost rather than a full assessment of their diversionary effectiveness (see Vanstone and Raynor 1981). Some of the unpublished research on day training (Willis 1979) provides useful evidence of diversion from custody, as well as persuasive arguments that the centres were cheaper than imprisonment.

For a more recent example, and one where evaluation is still continuing, we can turn to the Afan Alternative project in West Glamorgan. This project started in 1980 through the initiative of a probation officer who was also an experienced group worker, and aims to provide an alternative to custodial sentences for young adult male offenders aged 16 to 20. From the outset the objectives have involved both diversion and help, since the project aims not only to replace custodial sentences but also to provide a more constructive and helpful experience than the sentences it has replaced. The main method of work has been afternoon or evening groupwork sessions which combine physical training with the use of active techniques based on psychodrama and sociodrama to explore current and past problems in members' daily lives, and the legal basis involves an additional condition in probation orders or juvenile supervision orders requiring attendance at these sessions. This requirement is limited to the first six to nine months of the order, and required attendance has not exceeded six hours a week; contact is maintained with families through home visits. Thus the project involves far less restriction of liberty than the control unit model and incorporates a quite different attitude to offenders' needs. Systematic evaluation of the project was built in from the beginning through local initiatives, as no provision (perhaps surprisingly) had been made for research in the Home Office's allocation of funds to the experimental stage of the project. Evaluation has involved regular feedback to the project, and readers interested in full details of the evaluative material so far, and in more operational information about the project itself, will find this in the project reports (Lewis, Jones, Price and Lewis 1983; Raynor 1984). However, some of the detail is worth reviewing here to illustrate the attempt to combine diversion and help, and the extent to which fairly simple measures can throw light on the achievement of these objectives.

First, then, diversion. Over the first three years of the project's life, custodial sentencing of young male adults aged 17 to 20 in the magistrates' court declined from 24 per cent of all sentences (for offences other than minor motoring) to 11 per cent, while probation orders incorporating the project requirements rose to 9 per cent of disposals. 'Normal' probation, at 3 to 5 per cent, and community service at 7 to 8 per cent remained fairly constant, as did other non-custodial sentences. This reduction in custodial sentencing reversed a previous trend, and was not duplicated in other local courts or nationally. In respect of the project's main target group at the lower end of the adult age range these figures were consistent with diversion from custody rather than 'net-widening' diversion from other non-custodial disposals. Over the same period the office caseload, in which statutory after-care originally almost outweighed probation work, changed to 43 per cent probation orders, 24 per cent supervision orders and only 12 per cent statutory after-care. Corresponding national figures at the end of

1982 were 32 per cent probation, 10 per cent supervision and 21 per cent statutory after-care, and although the shortening of some licences by legislation in May 1983 may have improved the local figures slightly, the emerging pattern is what would be expected in an area where diversion is practised.

The previous histories of project members confirmed the 'heavy end' emphasis: with an average age of 18 years, the first 49 project members had an average of 5.6 previous convictions and 17 of them had already served custodial sentences, sometimes more than one. They were, in fact, slightly more heavily convicted than the average inmate of the nearest youth custody centre, and the distribution of previous convictions was comparable to that for receptions into custody nationally (see table 1).

TABLE 1   Distribution of previous convictions

	Less than 3 previous (%)	3—5 previous (%)	6 or more previous (%)
Males 17—20 receiving custodial sentences in 1981 (Home Office 1982)	29	37	34
Project members (N = 49)	14	45	41

It is interesting to note that of the 22 clients whose histories are detailed in the Kent Control Unit report, ten had fewer previous convictions than the average Afan project member, despite their average age, at 24 years, being much higher.

Thus the criminal histories of project members provide further evidence of diversion. Not surprisingly, their reconviction rate (currently 41 per cent within one year of sentence) is also comparable with similar offenders receiving custodial sentences (47 per cent of all young male adults released from Prison Department establishments in 1978 were convicted again within one year), but about half of those reconvicted received non-custodial sentences and remained with or returned to the project, and the public appears to be no less successfully protected than it would be by custodial sentencing.

In an attempt to provide some monitoring of the project's helping aims, all members are asked to complete a Mooney Problem Checklist at the beginning and end of their period of required attendance. This is administered by a researcher who is not a member of the project staff and the content is kept confidential. Of the 31 members for whom these data are available at the time of writing, 18 reported fewer problems after than before, 12 more and 1 the same. While this is not evidence that the improvements are *attributable* to the project, the continuing economic recession in the area and the previous life-styles of most project members would not encourage optimism about spontaneous improvement. Those who reported a reduction in problems were also less likely to be reconvicted, and it will be interesting to see if this trend is maintained.

To return to more general issues, this project appears so far to offer one example of relatively effective diversion and help through enhanced probation without the use of daily containment. Its disciplined approach to compliance with requirements is balanced by an emphasis on informed choice and clear agreements before acceptance on the project, and by a very explicit approach to the presentation of these issues in court; indeed, sentencers have been involved in the design and administration of the project by way of a voluntary management committee which has also included representatives from the local police, the social services department, the probation service, the nearest youth custody centre, the local university and local solicitors. This capacity to draw on a wide range of local support and expertise has been an important factor;

another has been a very careful approach to 'gatekeeping' which has ensured that virtually all potential recruits coming to the attention of the local probation service have been assessed for referral (although there may still be some 'leakage' into custody through other agencies). At the same time, temptations to 'widen the net' and accept lower-tariff referrals have been resisted. The importance of effective referral systems in 'alternative to custody' projects is underlined by experience elsewhere: for instance, the Manchester and Wiltshire 'multi-facility' schemes, which aimed to incorporate comprehensive packages of community resources into probation orders, suffered from a low level of referral, with one senior officer commenting: 'I have never been convinced of the value of packages' (Crow, Pease and Hillary 1980). Similarly, 10 of the 26 officers eligible to make referrals to the Probation Control Unit in Kent never did so. The value of effective referral procedures receives further confirmation from the series of juvenile justice system studies carried out by the Centre for Youth, Crime and Community at Lancaster University (Thorpe, Smith, Green and Paley 1980; Thorpe, Green and Smith 1980), which consistently show that sentencers' overreliance on custodial sentences and care orders is largely attributable not to their punitive instincts but to the failure of social workers to develop opportunities for non-custodial supervision and to use social inquiry reports systematically to attract referrals. Where such research has led to the introduction of consciously diversionary juvenile justice policies the results have been impressive, and if diversion requires the acceptance of additional conditions in court orders there seems a strong case for doing this, subject to the kind of safeguards against overintervention and drift which are outlined in this chapter.

Attention to what goes on around and across the boundaries of a project, as well as what happens inside it, raises again the issue of community links and community participation. The earlier discussion of modern criminal justice systems identified displacement of community participation as one of their unintended effects, and as a possible contributor to general frustration. By contrast, successful diversionary projects often involve and encourage a degree of community participation, and this is also a feature of other community initiatives in criminal justice such as victim support and reparation schemes. Recently the Home Office has encouraged probation services to think more actively about community involvement in the problem of crime, and here again the kind of principles stated at the beginning of this chapter may prove relevant. For instance, in the draft version of the Home Office paper on objectives and priorities for the probation service, the issue of community involvement was introduced under the heading of 'crime reduction', a notoriously elusive goal in relation to which it is always difficult to measure effectiveness. Crime prevention through community development seems in practice to require particularly broadly based and indirect initiatives, involving local people in a wide range of community activities informed by their own perceptions of the problems of their neighbourhood (as in the Cunningham Road Improvement Scheme pioneered by NACRO in the late seventies — Spence and Hedges 1976). It is by no means clear that the probation service is currently well equipped to undertake this kind of work; neither the experience and training of most of its staff, nor its status as a statutory agency, nor its traditional focus on what happens to offenders *after* they commit crimes seem to suggest that it could quickly gear itself to the effective pursuit of crime prevention through community development. Social services departments, with their more explicit preventive role in relation to social problems, may in theory be better placed, but in practice other needs are likely to take priority, particularly given the state of local government finance in the forseeable future. However, the development of community strategies to cope more constructively with the *consequences* of crime seems more feasible, and could be pursued in a manner consistent with the principles outlined at the beginning of this chapter.

This would imply, for instance, an active approach to the development of victim support, as a way of increasing community involvement in criminal justice problems as well as a means of helping some victims. More directly, it would imply support for the development of reparation schemes: for instance, Martin Wright's feasibility study of reparation in Coventry (1983) outlines the scope for a project which could involve significant displacement from more coercive sentences as well as direct benefits for victims. Again the principles of reducing coercion and increasing participation apply, perhaps with the additional implication that where wider participation can effectively shift criminal justice decisions in the direction of less coercion, this is more useful than promoting participation as an end in itself. So far there is little experience of reparation in Britain to show how far these complementary aims can be realised, but the results of the pioneering schemes in Coventry, Sheffield and elsewhere will be awaited with great interest.

For a final illustration of the possible links between community participation and reducing coercion in criminal justice, we return to the issue of alternatives to custody. A recent social inquiry report on a heavily convicted young offender in a small Welsh town offered a diversionary package (subject to consent by the defendant, his parents and various third parties, with the offer of regular progress reports to the court) which can be summarised as follows:

1 participation in an intermediate treatment group programme weekly;
2 participation in community service activities carried out by the intermediate treatment group;
3 reparation to the victims of his burglaries (several of whom had consented to his carrying out up to 50 hours work at their premises, under supervision, and the local police superintendent had also

'expressed cautious approval subject to adequate supervision');

4　a work experience programme arranged through the careers officer of the Manpower Services Commission;

5　referral for psychiatric investigation in relation to a long-standing psychosomatic problem.

This programme (which the court accepted after contemplating a substantial custodial sentence) involved the active participation of the defendant; the court; his parents; the other members of the intermediate treatment group; the beneficiaries of the community service work; the victims; the volunteers who supervised the work; the police; the careers officer; and the psychiatrist, in addition of course to the officer himself. All participated on a clearly agreed basis. This would have been impossible without some years of work in the community by the particular probation officer, but it offers an interesting illustration, not of some vague notion of 'community involvement' but of the purposeful mobilisation of community resources to resolve a criminal justice problem in a fair and helpful way.

11

Unfinished Theory and Critical Practice

As this has been a book about social work in the criminal justice system, it has necessarily concentrated on the probation service and the kind of work that service does or could do. However, I would suggest that much of the argument is directly transferable to other social work services, such as social services departments, which share a responsibility for parts of the criminal justice process. I have portrayed social workers as having more potential influence than actual power, and the proposed strategies therefore concentrate on providing opportunities for decision-making systems to move in a more humane direction, rather than on ways of forcing them to do so. Some elements of this approach may be transferable to the work that social workers do around other decision-making systems which affect their clients' interests, such as the allocation of welfare benefits or housing; for instance, the explicit emphasis on setting and monitoring objectives in relation to changes in systems as well as changes in clients could have a variety of applications wherever the attention of social workers ranges beyond the presumed pathology of individuals. However, as far as criminal justice is concerned the proposed strategies are aimed at improvement rather than transformation; large parts of the system will remain harsh and coercive, and the attempt to explore interests which victim and offender have in common will often be frustrated by discovering that they perceive none at all. In a society which seems to be becoming more unequal and more authoritarian, ideas about less coercive criminal justice may seem particularly untimely; but such a view perhaps underestimates other forces, and the aspiration to a more humane system of justice should be seen as part of the general case for a greater respect for persons and a greater collective commitment to welfare.

Nor are the proposed strategies concerned solely with accommodation and compromise. While they involve integrative methods such as creating more opportunities for sentencers to make helpful decisions, they can also incorporate more aggressive tactics; for instance, some intermediate treatment workers have followed a policy of encouraging appeals against custodial sentences, using the higher courts to reverse the decisions of local magistrates (Johnson, O'Hanlon and Mulcahy 1984). The test of such tactics is whether they are effective in pursuing appropriate objectives. While there is often a strong case for preferring the methods of rational persuasion, the criminal justice system is not rational and in some respects it is out of control, consistently producing outcomes which hardly anybody wants. Any system which allows the introduction of harsher regimes as an experiment in two detention centres without any reason to expect that this will be effective, sets up research to find out if it is, and then extends the regime to two more centres before the research is complete, seems somewhat lacking in rationality; now that the new regime is to be extended to still more centres even *after* the research has shown it to be ineffective (Young Offender Psychology Unit 1984), plain common sense detects some craziness.

Any attempts to promote change in such a system must be varied, creative and provisional. They may not succeed, in which case something else must be tried; practitioners must be both committed and sceptical, cultivating the skills of simultaneous involvement and detachment, acting with conviction at the same time as trying to find out if they are wrong. Halmos's principle of 'equilibration', the disciplined use of uncertainty, is echoed in the criminal justice field by Mathiesen's notion of 'the unfinished' (1974); strategies for change in criminal justice must, he argues, resist defining themselves as either reformist or radical, since reformist strategies can be co-opted to reinforce existing arrangements and radical strategies can be 'defined out' as subversive. What matters is that they should move in the right direction on the basis of unfinished and provisional theory and constant critical evaluation of their practice. This will disappoint those readers who like to allocate ideas to neat closed ideological compartments; however, to be theoretically unfinished is better than to be theoretically finished and practically irrelevant.

Maintaining a state of unfinished theory, critical practice and disciplined learning has implications for training and management in agencies. It requires the development and cultivation of a critical culture which can allow broad agreement on medium-term goals to coexist with constant questioning of routine policy and practice and with the encouragement of initiatives from below as well as above. This will be uncomfortable for those managers, if they exist, who prefer the predictable safety of bureaucracies, and for those staff, if they exist, who find it convenient to combine a highly critical view of management with a generously uncritical view of themselves. These, however, are matters for agencies and practitioners to sort out, and lie beyond the scope of this book. What I have tried to show is simply that possibilities for change exist, that desirable directions of change can be identified and that some changes are not only desirable but feasible. Of course, the principles of critical practice apply also to academic onlookers: we are never more open to correction than when we think we have something useful to say.

References

Adams S. (1961), 'Interaction between individual interview therapy and treatment amenability in older youth authority wards', in *Inquiries Concerning Kinds of Treatment for Kinds of Offenders*, California Board of Corrections.

Adams S. (1967), 'Some findings from correctional caseload research' *Federal Probation*, vol. 31, no. 4.

Advisory Council on the Penal System (1974), *Young Adult Offenders*, HMSO.

Alfero L. A. (1972), 'Conscientization' in *New Themes in Social Work Education* (proceedings of the XVIth International Congress of Schools of Social Work), International Association of Schools of Social Work.

American Friends' Service Committee (1971), *Struggle for Justice*, Hill & Wang.

Bailey R. and Brake M. (eds) (1975), *Radical Social Work*, Edward Arnold.

Barclay P. M. (1982), chairman, *Social Workers: their Role and Tasks* Bedford Square Press.

Barkdull W. L. (1976), 'Probation: call it control — and mean it', *Federal Probation*, vol. 43, no. 4.

Bean P. (1976), *Rehabilitation and Deviance*, Routledge & Kegan Paul.

Beaumont B. (1976), 'A supportive role' *Probation Journal*, vol. 23, no. 3.

Becker H. S. (1963), *Outsiders*, Free Press of Glencoe.

Becker H. S. (1973), 'Labelling theory reconsidered', in Becker H. S., *Outsiders*, revised edition, Free Press.

Benn S. I. (1967), 'Freedom and persuasion', *Australasian Journal of Philosophy*, vol. 45, reprinted in McDermott F. E. (1975) (ed.), *Self-Determination in Social Work*, Routledge & Kegan Paul.

Berger P. (1976), *Pyramids of Sacrifice*, Penguin.

Blagg H. and Derricourt N. (forthcoming), *Evaluation of Corby Juvenile Liaison Bureau 1982—4*, Department of Social Administration, Lancaster University.

Bottoms A. E. (1980), *The Suspended Sentence after Ten Years*, Centre for Social Work and Applied Social Studies, University of Leeds.

Bottoms A. E. and McWilliams W. (1979), 'A non-treatment paradigm for probation practice' *British Journal of Social Work*, vol. 9, no. 2.

Brake M. and Bailey R. (1980), *Radical Social Work and Practice*, E. Arnold.

Brandt R. B. (1976), 'The concept of welfare' in Timms N. and Watson D. (eds), *Talking about Welfare*, Routledge & Kegan Paul.

Brody S. R. (1976), *The Effectiveness of Sentencing*, HMSO.

Bryant M., Coker J., Estlea B., Himmel S. and Knapp T. (1978), 'Sentenced to social work', *Probation Journal*, vol. 25, no. 4.

Burnham D. (1981), 'The new orthodoxy', *Probation Journal*, vol. 28, no. 4.

Burton J. W. (1969), *Conflict and Communication*, Macmillan.

Burton J. W. (1979), *Deviance, Terrorism and War*, Martin Robertson.

Carlen P. (1976), *Magistrates' Justice*, Martin Robertson.

Case Con Collective (1971), 'Statement of aims', unpublished.

Chapman J. (1977), 'Defining the vital tasks', *Probation Journal*, vol. 24, no. 1.

Christie N. (1977), 'Conflicts as property', *British Journal of Criminology*, vol. 17, no. 1.

Christie N. (1982), *Limits to Pain*, Martin Robertson.

Cicourel A. V. (1968), *The Social Organization of Juvenile Justice*, Wiley.

Cohen S. (1979), 'The punitive city: notes on the dispersal of social control', *Contemporary Crises*, vol. 3, no. 4.

Corrigan P. and Leonard P. (1978), *Social Work Practice under Capitalism*, Macmillan.

Critcher C. (1976), 'Structures, cultures and biographies' in Hall S. and Jefferson T. (eds), *Resistance through Rituals*, Hutchinson.

Croft J. (1978), *Research in Criminal Justice*, HMSO.

Crow I., Pease K and Hillary M. (1980) *The Manchester and Wiltshire Multifacility Schemes,* NACRO.

Davies M. (1974), *Social Work in the Environment,* HMSO.

Davies M. (1979), 'Through the eyes of the probationer', *Probation Journal,* vol. 26, no. 4.

Davies M. (1981), *The Essential Social Worker,* Heinemann.

Davies M. (1982), 'Community-based alternatives to custody: the right place for the probation service', unpublished address to a conference of chief probation officers.

Day P. (1983), 'Consumer and supervisor perspectives on probation', *Probation Journal,* vol. 30, no. 2.

DHSS (1974), *Report of the Committee of Inquiry into the Care and Supervision Provided in Relation to Maria Colwell,* HMSO.

Downie R. S. and Telfer E. (1969), *Respect for Persons,* Allen & Unwin.

Downie R. S. and Telfer E. (1980), *Caring and Curing,* Methuen.

Drakeford M. (1983), 'Probation: containment or liberty?', *Probation Journal,* vol. 30, no. 1.

Eysenck H. J. (1966), *The Effects of Psychotherapy,* International Science Press.

Fischer J. (1976), *The Effectiveness of Social Casework,* Charles C. Thomas.

Flew A. (1973), *Crime or Disease?,* Macmillan.

Folkard M. S., Smith D. E. and Smith D. D. (1976), *IMPACT Vol II: the Results of the Experiment,* HMSO.

Foren R. and Bailey R. (1968), *Authority in Social Casework,* Pergamon Press.

Freire P. (1972), *Pedagogy of the Oppressed,* Penguin.

Gleeson D. (1974), 'Theory and practice in the sociology of Paulo Freire', *Radical Philosophy,* 8 (summer).

Goldberg E. M. and Stanley S. J. (1979), 'A task-centred approach to probation' in King J. F. S. (ed.), *Pressures and Change in the Probation Service,* Cambridge Institute of Criminology.

Gostin L. (1977), *A Human Condition,* MIND.

Griffiths W. A. (1982), 'Supervision in the community', *Justice of the Peace,* 21 August.

Habermas J. (1976), *Legitimation Crisis,* Heinemann.

Hall P. (1976), *Reforming the Welfare,* Heinemann.

Hall S., Clarke J., Critcher C., Jefferson T. and Roberts B. (1978), *Policing the Crisis*, Macmillan.

Halmos P. (1978), *The Personal and the Political*, Hutchinson.

Handler J. (1973), *The Coercive Social Worker*, Academic Press.

Hardiker P. (1977), 'Social work ideologies in the probation service', *British Journal of Social Work*, vol. 7, no. 2.

Harding J. (1982), *Victims and Offenders*, Bedford Square Press.

Harris R. J. (1977), 'The probation officer as social worker', *British Journal of Social Work*, vol. 7, no. 4.

Harris R. J. (1980), 'A changing service: the case for separating care and control in probation practice', *British Journal of Social Work*, vol. 10, no. 2.

Haxby D. (1978), *Probation: a Changing Service*, Constable.

Hine J., McWilliams W. and Pease K. (1978), 'Recommendations, social information and sentencing', *Howard Journal*, vol. 17, no. 2.

Hinton N. (1976), 'Developments in the probation service', *Probation Journal*, vol. 23, no. 3.

Hollis F. (1968), *A Typology of Casework Treatment*, Family Service Association (New York).

Home Office (1968), *Children in Trouble*, Cmnd 3601, HMSO.

Home Office (1969), *The Sentence of the Court*, HMSO.

Home Office (1980), *Young Offenders*, Cmnd 8045, HMSO.

Home Office (1981a), *Probation and After-Care Statistics England and Wales 1980*.

Home Office (1981b), *The Brixton Disorders 10–12 April 1981*, Report of an Inquiry by the Rt. Hon. The Lord Scarman O.B.E., Cmnd 8427, HMSO.

Home Office (1982), *Prison Statistics England and Wales 1981*, HMSO.

Home Office (1983), *The British Crime Survey: First Report* (by M. Hough and P. Mayhew), HMSO.

Home Office (1984), *Probation Service in England and Wales: Statement of National Objectives and Priorities*.

Hood R. (1966), 'A study of the effectiveness of pre-sentence investigations in reducing recidivism', *British Journal of Criminology*, vol. 6, no. 3.

Hood R. (1974), *Tolerance and the Tariff*, NACRO.

Hood R. and Sparks R. (1970), *Key Issues in Criminology*, World University Library.

Howe D. (1980), 'Inflated states and empty theories in social work', *British Journal of Social Work*, vol. 10, no. 3.

Hulsman L. (1983), 'Civilizing criminal justice', address to the Annual Conference of the Howard League, unpublished.

Hume D. (1740), *A Treatise of Human Nature*, book III, Thomas Longman.

Hunt A. W. (1964), 'Enforcement in probation casework', *British Journal of Criminology*, vol. 4, no. 3.

Jaffe H. J. (1979), 'Probation with a flair', *Federal Probation*, vol. 43, no. 1.

Jarman D. (1974), 'Younger or better?', *Probation Journal*, vol. 21, no. 4.

Johnson T., O'Hanlon F. and Mulcahy A. (1984), 'A second opinion', *Community Care*, 19 April.

Jordan W. (1975), 'Is your client a fellow citizen?', *Social Work Today,* vol. 6, no. 15.

Kellmer Pringle M. (1974), *The Needs of Children,* Hutchinson.

Kent Probation and After-Care Service (1981), 'Probation Control Unit: a community based experiment in intensive supervision', *Annual Report on the Work of the Medway Centre,* Kent Probation and After-Care Service.

Kent Probation Service (1982), *The Kent Probation Control Unit: the First Year of Operation,* Development, Information and Training Unit, Kent Probation Service.

King J. F. S. (1979) (ed.), *Pressures and Change in the Probation Service,* Cambridge Institute of Criminology.

Lea J. and Young J. (1984), *What is to be Done about Law and Order?*, Penguin.

Lemert E. (1967), *Human Deviance, Social Problems and Social Control,* Prentice-Hall.

Leonard P. (1975), 'Towards a paradigm for radical practice' in Bailey R. and Brake M. (eds), *Radical Social Work*, Edward Arnold.

Leonard P. (1976), 'The function of social work in society' in Timms N. and Watson D. (eds), *Talking about Welfare*, Routledge & Kegan Paul.

Lewis, D., Jones H., Price H. and Lewis M. (1983), *The Afan Alternative,* West Glamorgan Probation Service.

Lipton D., Martinson R. and Wilks J. (1975), *The Effectiveness of Correctional Treatment*, Praeger Publishers.

Lukes S. (1974), *Power: a Radical View*, Macmillan.

Maguire M. (1980), 'The impact of burglary upon victims', *British Journal of Criminology*, vol. 20, no. 3.

Marcuse H. (1964), *One-Dimensional Man,* Routledge & Kegan Paul.

Martinson R. (1974), 'What works?', *The Public Interest*, New York, March.

Maslow A. H. (1954), *Motivation and Personality,* Harper Bros.

Mathiesen T. (1974), *The Politics of Abolition,* Martin Robertson.

Matza D. (1969), *Becoming Deviant*, Prentice-Hall.

Mayer J. E. and Timms N. (1970), *The Client Speaks*, Routledge & Kegan Paul.

McWilliams W. (1981), 'The probation officer at court: from friend to acquaintance', *Howard Journal*, vol. 20, no. 2.

Mead G. H. (1934), *Mind, Self and Society,* University of Chicago Press.

Meyer H. J., Borgatta E. F. and Jones W. C. (1965), *Girls at Vocational High,* Russell Sage Foundation.

Mill J. S. (1859), *On Liberty*, London.

Mills C. W. (1943), 'The professional ideology of social pathologists', *American Journal of Sociology*, vol. 49, no. 2.

Monger M. (1964), *Casework in Probation*, Butterworth.

Morgan P. (1978), *Delinquent Fantasies*, Temple Smith.

Morris A., Giller H., Szwed E. and Geach H. (1980), *Justice for Children,* Macmillan.

Morrissey M. and Pease K. (1982), 'The black criminal justice system in west Belfast', *Howard Journal*, vol. 21, no. 3.

NAPO (1981), *The Provision of Alternatives to Custody and the Use of the Probation Order,* National Association of Probation Officers.

NAVSS (1984), *Fourth Annual Report*, National Association of Victims Support Schemes.

NMAG (1976), *Working Document*, NAPO Members' Action Group.

Nottinghamshire Probation Service (1984), *Observations on Whatton Detention Centre Discharges (Juveniles) 1983.*

One-Parent Families (1982), *Against Natural Justice*, One-Parent Families.

Palmer T. (1974), 'The youth authority's community treatment project', *Federal Probation*, vol. 38, no. 1.

Parker H. (1974), *View from the Boys*, David & Charles.

Parkinson L. (1983), 'Conciliation', *British Journal of Social Work*, vol. 13, no. 1.

Pearson G. (1975), *The Deviant Imagination*, Macmillan.

Pease K. and McWilliams W. (1980), *Community Service by Order*, Scottish Academic Press.

Perlman H. H. (1957), *Social Casework: a Problem-Solving Process*, University of Chicago Press.

Perry F. C. (1974), *Information for the Court*, Cambridge Institute of Criminology.

Pincus A. and Minahan A. (1973), *Social Work Practice: Model and Method*, F. E. Peacock.

Plant R. (1970), *Social and Moral Theory in Casework*, Routledge & Kegan Paul.

Powers E. and Witmer H. (1951), *An Experiment in the Treatment of Delinquency*, Columbia University Press.

Radzinowicz L. (1958), *The Results of Probation*, Macmillan.

Raynor P. (1978), 'Compulsory persuasion: a problem for correctional social work', *British Journal of Social Work*, vol. 8, no. 4.

Raynor P. (1981), 'Diagnosis and description: who owns the problem?', *Probation Journal*, vol. 28, no. 2.

Raynor P. (1982), 'Control Power', *Social Work Today*, vol. 13, no. 19.

Raynor P. (1984), *An Alternative to Custody for Young Offenders: the First Three Years of the Afan Alternative Project*, School of Social Studies, University College of Swansea.

Reid W. J. and Epstein L. (1972), *Task-Centred Casework*, Columbia University Press.

Rex J. (1961), *Key Problems in Sociological Theory*, Routledge & Kegan Paul.

Roberts S. (1979), *Order and Dispute: an Introduction to Legal Anthropology*, Penguin.

Romig D. A. (1978), *Justice for Our Children: an Examination of Juvenile Delinquent Rehabilitation Programs*, Lexington Books.

Rosenhan D. L. (1973), 'On being sane in insane places', *Science,* 19 January.

Sartre J. P. (1952), *Saint Genet, Comédien et Martyr*, Librairie Gallimard.

Saunders P. (1980), *Urban Politics,* Penguin.

Scheff T. J. (1966), *Being Mentally Ill,* Aldine.

Seebohm F. (1968), chairman, *Report of the Committee on Local Authority and Allied Personal Services*, Cmnd 3703, HMSO.

Serge V. (1969), *Men in Prison,* Doubleday.

Shapland J. (1982), 'The victim in the criminal justice system', *Home Office Research Bulletin*, no. 14.

Shaw M. (1974), *Social Work in Prison,* HMSO.

Smith D. et al. (1984), *Reducing the Prison Population*, Home Office Research and Planning Unit Paper 23, HMSO.

Smith G. (1980), *Social Need*, Routledge & Kegan Paul.

Spence J. and Hedges A. (1976), *Community Planning Project: Cunningham Road Improvement Scheme Interim Report*, Social and Community Planning Research.

Strawson P. F. (1968), 'Freedom and resentment' in Strawson (ed.), *Studies in the Philosophy of Thought and Action*, Oxford University Press.

Sutton C. (1979), *Psychology for Social Workers and Counsellors*, Routledge & Kegan Paul.

Sylvester S. F. (1977), 'The dilemma of the correctional idea', *Federal Probation*, vol. 41, no. 2.

Taylor I. (1981), *Law and Order: Arguments for Socialism*, Macmillan.

Taylor L., Lacey R. and Bracken D. (1980), *In Whose Best Interests?*, Cobden Trust/MIND.

Thomas D. (1964), 'Theories of punishment in the court of criminal appeal', *Modern Law Review*, vol. 27, September.

Thorpe D. H., Green C. and Smith D. (1980), *Punishment and Welfare*, Department of Social Administration, University of Lancaster.

Thorpe D. H., Smith D., Green C. J. and Paley J. (1980), *Out of Care: the Community Support of Juvenile Offenders,* Allen & Unwin.

Thorpe J. and Pease K. (1976), 'The relationship between recommendations made to the court and sentences passed', *British Journal of Criminology,* vol. 16, no. 4.

Truax C. and Carkhuff R. R. (1967), *Toward Effective Counselling and Psychotherapy*, Aldine.

Turnbull C. (1973), *The Mountain People*, Jonathan Cape.

Vanstone M. (1985), 'Moving away from help: policy and practice in probation day centres', *Howard Journal*, vol. 24, no. 1.

Vanstone M. (forthcoming), 'The Pontypridd day training centre: diversion from prison in action' in Poynting J. E. (ed.), *Alternatives to Custody*, Basil Blackwell.

Vanstone M. and Raynor P. (1981), 'Diversion from prison: a partial success and a missed opportunity', *Probation Journal*, vol. 28, no. 3.

Von Wright G. H. (1963), *The Varieties of Goodness*, Routledge & Kegan Paul.

Walker H. and Beaumont B. (1981), *Probation Work: Critical Theory and Socialist Practice*, Basil Blackwell.

Watson D. (1980), *Caring for Strangers*, Routledge & Kegan Paul.

Wilkins L. T. (1964), *Social Deviance*, Tavistock.

Willis A. (1979), 'Displacement from custody: a review of the day training experiment' in *Pontypridd Day Training Centre Evaluation Report*, Mid-Glamorgan Probation Service, unpublished.

Willis A. (1981), *Effective Criminal Supervision towards New Standards and Goals*, lecture to NAPO branch day conference at Dartington, unpublished.

Willis A. (1983), 'The balance between care and control in probation: a research note', *British Journal of Social Work*, vol. 13, no. 3.

Wilson E. (1977), *Women and the Welfare State*, Tavistock.

Wootton B. (1959), *Social Science and Social Pathology*, Allen & Unwin.

Wright M. (1982), *Making Good: Prisons, Punishment and Beyond*, Burnett Books.

Wright M. (1983), *Victim/Offender Reparation Agreements: a Feasibility Study in Coventry*, West Midlands Probation Service.

Young J. (1971), *The Drugtakers*, Paladin.

Young Offender Psychology Unit (1984), *Tougher Regimes in Detention Centres*, HMSO.

Index